I CAN'T BELIEVE IT'S BABY FOOD!

I CAN'T BELIEVE IT'S BABY FOOD!

LUCINDA MILLER

Dedicated to Archie & Edward

Published in 2021 by Short Books, an imprint of Octopus Publishing Group Ltd
Carmelite House, 50 Victoria Embankment London, EC4Y 0DZ
www.octopusbooks.co.uk www.shortbooks.co.uk

An Hachette UK Company www.hachette.co.uk

10 9 8 7 6 5 4 3 2

Copyright © Lucinda Miller 2021

A CIP catalogue record for this book is available from the British Library.

ISBN: 978-1-78072-476-8
Project editor: Jo Roberts-Miller
Cover and book design by Smith & Gilmour
Photography copyright © Smith & Gilmour
Food stylist: Lola Milne

Printed in China

FSC
www.fsc.org
MIX
Paper | Supporting
responsible forestry
FSC® C008047

CONTENTS

INTRODUCTION 7

✳

✳

INTRODUCTION

Feeding your baby or toddler is one of the messiest and most time-consuming parts of parenthood. But it can also be a hugely fun and rewarding experience. It's a chance to introduce your child to so many exciting smells, colours, flavours and textures from our wonderful planet, and to spark a lasting love of healthy food, with all the physical and mental health benefits that this provides.

My clinical work is dedicated to helping children develop into the best versions of themselves, and nutrition is at the heart of this. There are few better feelings as a parent than watching your child tucking into food that is good for them; and one of the best things you can do as your baby comes through the weaning stage is to arm yourself with a repertoire of easy, nutritious recipes which you know they will enjoy. But eating is a very social activity. Babies and young children develop their relationship with food from you. So, it is also important to sit down and eat with them as much as you can.

This is why I have written *I Can't Believe it's Baby Food!* My aim is to help parents make both cooking and mealtimes as enjoyable and stress-free as possible. It's all about sharing food that the whole family will love, with your baby in a highchair pulled up to the table. Apart from the first few weeks of weaning, there really is no need to cook twice. Indeed, it's much better that you

don't! Your baby will benefit both nutritionally and developmentally from eating with you; and, if you are not stuck in the kitchen all day preparing endless different meals, you'll be happier and less frazzled, too.

People are often surprised when I say that babies and toddlers can eat pretty much anything that older children and adults eat – it's as if our food were different in some way, filled with ingredients and flavours that could be off-putting for a baby, or perhaps even bad for them.

Of course, you need to use some caution and judgement. There are certain foods that should not be given to a baby before they turn one; and you need to introduce new foods and flavours gradually. But as a general rule, once your baby is through the early weaning stage (around 6 months), offering them an unsalted, softened version of your healthy meal will do them nothing but good.

All my recipes are based on the most up-to-date weaning guidelines and early years nutrition research, and have a focus on feeding your little one's immune system, brain development and gut microbiome, which are now known to be three critical foundations for their future health, happiness and development.

Every bite is supercharged with flavour and nourishment. I have added a healthy twist to many traditional nursery foods and included flavours from all around the world. My mission is to create a generation of little foodies, who embrace a diverse range of food types, tastes and cuisines. And, who knows? You might discover some new food favourites yourself in the process! All the recipes can be adapted to suit the taste buds of older children and adults and be integrated into family meals and snacks – it's just as important for parents to feed themselves food that is healthy as it is for their children, and they should not put themselves at the bottom of the pile.

Having specialised in clinical child nutrition for over 20 years, I have seen first-hand which aspects of children's eating parents tend to find most challenging; so I have started this recipe book with a section covering the facts, to explain the things you should be doing and the science behind them. I have tried to answer the questions that are most commonly asked by parents in clinic and increasingly on social media. This includes guidelines on optimal nourishment for babies with food restrictions, such as dairy, egg or nut allergies. And, as with my previous cookbook for older children, *The Good Stuff*, I include clever allergen swaps,

so you can adapt any recipe to suit your child's specific dietary needs. I am also increasingly asked to provide nutrition advice for vegetarian and vegan families, or for those simply wanting to cut back on consuming animal products. So, I have included a section on this, which gives you the tools and know-how to ensure your baby does not miss out on any key nutrients. The majority of my recipes are either plant-based already or can be easily adapted to be meat-, fish-, egg- or dairy-free.

Many of the recipes are the winners from when I was weaning my own three children, as well as the favourites enjoyed by my nephews, nieces and little clinic clients. I have been lucky to have been given some cooking gems from Marion Boulter, a qualified nutritional therapist who is an important part of my NatureDoc clinical team, the mother of two gorgeous young boys and a qualified chef who has taught at the Tante Marie cookery school. I have also reached out to the thousands of parents in my NatureDoc online community, to ensure that this is the most nutritious, practical, healthy, creative AND delicious baby and toddler cookbook ever.

Have fun rolling up your sleeves and getting busy in the kitchen!

WHY IS A HEALTHY DIET SO IMPORTANT FOR GROWING CHILDREN?

It is well established that the first 1,000 days of a child's life (from conception through to their second birthday) is the most critical window for providing the nutrient building blocks for their future health. The wrong food choices during this early developmental period can increase risk factors for a range of health issues and diseases, including obesity, type 2 diabetes, childhood cancers, autism and dyslexia[1], as well as mood problems including depression[2] and anxiety[3]. Sadly, many of these conditions are on the rise[4].

On the other hand, a healthy diet positively influences learning, focus and behaviour, as well as good self-esteem and self-confidence[5]. It can also help to manage or prevent common health challenges like eczema[6], allergies[7], asthma[8] and constipation[9]. Innate intelligence can also be affected by diet. Research has found that a diet high in processed sugary foods can reduce a child's IQ by the time they are eight years old, while a healthy diet full of fresh food can actually increase their IQ[10].

The biggest driver behind all the diet-related health issues of today seems to be the rise of ultra-processed food and this now fills over 50% of our shopping trollies. The growth of the baby food industry is a large part of this convenience culture, as more and more parents turn to pouches, jars and packets rather than cooking from scratch.

Shop-bought baby food tends to be very low in iron, protein and essential fatty acids and very high in fruit and refined grains, which are not good for the metabolism and can set up a sweet tooth. The crunchy snacks may not have much sugar on the label, but are made from grains like rice and corn that give a big sugar hit and they set up a love of 'crunch', which can be a big reason why older kids get hooked on crisps.

I'm not saying never grab a pouch or feed them a rice cake, as they are extremely helpful when out and about; but maybe aim to use them only about 20% of the time.

Home cooking not only gives your child a better start to life from a nutritional point of view, but also exposes them to the wide range of tastes, textures and the smells of home cooking that shop bought food can never match! It sets up their taste buds for a life-long love of different foods.

MY SIMPLE FOOD MANTRAS

✳ Cook from scratch as much as possible and choose the best quality ingredients you can afford. This clearly means bypassing the convenience food aisles in your supermarket.

✳ Keep within the NHS guidelines for sugar intake and cut back on ingredients with a high glycaemic value – e.g. white flour and refined starches which can give your child an even bigger sugar spike than table sugar[11].

✳ 5 types of fruits and veg a day should be a bare minimum. I understand that this is one of the hardest challenges for parents. But even if your little one is a champion veg dodger, I'll show you how to ensure they get the nutrients they need by hiding veg in smoothies, ice lollies, sauces, pancakes and waffles, until they grow out of fussy eating and start enjoying their greens.

✳ Eat a good balance of protein, fat and carbohydrate. Kids tend to love their carbs and it can be harder to get them to eat healthy fats and protein. This is why every recipe in this book combines a bit of each of these.

✳ Adopt a wholefood diet, so the goodness hasn't been stripped from its original form. Choose wholegrain brown rice, pasta and bread over the white versions a few times a week for variety.

✳ Full-fat dairy[12] and eggs are back on the menu. These two foods were once demonised for being contributors to weight gain, heart disease and high cholesterol, but it has now been shown that consuming full-fat dairy products is actually associated with reduced risk of a child becoming overweight or obese and suffering from cardiovascular problems[13]. Eggs can also be eaten every day[14] and are a great source of protein, vitamins and minerals. Most importantly, foods made with these whole ingredients quite simply taste so much better!

✳ Make the food super-delicious and mealtimes fun. This is perhaps the most critical point of all, since pleasure and taste are such important factors in developing a healthy relationship with food[15]. If you manage to eat home-cooked food with good-quality ingredients 80% of the time, you're off to a great start. I've found over my years of clinical practice that getting this part of parenting right helps to prevent many health hurdles before they happen.

6 REASONS TO COOK FROM SCRATCH

① TASTE

A healthy, homemade meal with fresh ingredients tastes so good that it doesn't need flavour enhancers.

② TEXTURE

Home-cooked food varies in texture more than the processed stuff; the biggest reason kids become fussy is texture preference over taste, so getting them used to eating a range of textures early on really helps in the long term.

③ BETTER NUTRITION

Not only is homemade food naturally more nutritious and you are able to give more variety, but you also have the chance to adapt your baby's diet to suit their needs: more foods rich in vitamin C when unwell; more iron-rich foods when they are looking tired and pasty; more fibrous foods if constipated.

④ QUALITY CONTROL

Since you are the one buying the ingredients, you know exactly what's going into your baby's food.

⑤ CARE FOR THE ENVIRONMENT

You can reduce single use plastic if you avoid baby food pouches.

⑥ ECONOMY

Cooking in batches with good-quality ingredients can be a lot cheaper than buying ready-made baby food.

WHY BUY ORGANIC?

Even though UK and European farmers have been working hard to reduce pesticide use on their crops, this is still a factor we have to bear in mind when buying food for our children. Almost all baby food brands are now organic for a very good reason. Young children are more susceptible than adults to the health risks posed by exposure to too many pesticides because their organs are still developing and maturing[16].

Of course, not all non-organic foods are unsafe, far from it. But even low levels of pesticides can affect neurological and behavioural development. They can affect baby reflexes, coordination and dexterity. There is also a link between pesticide exposure and the development of childhood cancers[17], and pesticides have been cited as one of the causes of the rise in obesity[18] in children.

Pregnant women and breastfeeding mums should try and reduce their pesticide exposure[19,20], too, as the maternal toxic load can affect your little one.

With this in mind, please do your best to source organic ingredients as much as you can. This includes dairy produce, as well as fruits and vegetables. To give you an example, pesticides and antibiotics have been found in up to 60% of conventional milk, whereas none was found in organic[21].

Sometimes it is difficult or too expensive to source organic fruits and vegetables and, in this instance, I recommend washing and peeling non-organic fruits and veggies, or soaking them in some water with a heaped teaspoon of bicarbonate of soda[22] for 15 minutes to help clean off any pesticide residue or other impurities.

One way to keep costs down is to get savvy with knowing which fruits and veggies are likely to have pesticides lurking. Every year something called The Dirty Dozen is published online, which is a list of fruit and vegetables that tend to be sprayed the most with pesticides, so in these instances you gain more from choosing organic. Alongside this is The Clean Fifteen, a list of the fruits and veggies that are lowest in pesticide residue or that you peel anyway – so buying organic is less important.

THE DIRTY DOZEN

1. Strawberries	7. Peaches
2. Spinach	8. Cherries
3. Kale	9. Pears
4. Nectarines	10. Tomatoes
5. Apples	11. Celery
6. Grapes	12. Potatoes

THE CLEAN FIFTEEN

1. Avocado	9. Cauliflower
2. Sweetcorn	10. Cantaloupe melon
3. Pineapples	11. Broccoli
4. Onions	12. Mushrooms
5. Papaya	13. Cabbage
6. Frozen peas	14. Honeydew melon
7. Aubergine	15. Kiwi
8. Asparagus	

Source: EWG 2020 https://www.ewg.org/

WEANING & BABY NUTRITION MASTERCLASS

IS MY BABY READY TO WEAN?

Over the past 20 years while I have been a mum, the NHS guidelines[23] on when to introduce solid foods have swung several times between 4 and 6 months. The current recommendation is 6 months, since this works for most babies. However, there is some flexibility in timing and some babies can be ready either slightly sooner or later.

The earliest that solids can be introduced into a baby's diet is at 17 weeks of age, as their gut is simply not ready for solid food before this time. That said, waiting the full 26 weeks is by no means essential for all babies; indeed, there is one school of thought that weaning a little earlier than 6 months may help to prevent the development of food allergies[24], especially peanuts and eggs. If you have allergies in the family or feel that your child might be susceptible, this is something you should discuss with your paediatrician.

Many parents find that their baby starts to show signs of readiness for solid foods from around 4 months old – you may notice a little pair of eyes watching you intently when you are eating your toast in the morning. However, instead of going all in immediately, my advice is that you wait until you see a whole collection of signs.

Your baby is ready to start eating solid food when they have:

✳ Good head control and are able to maintain a sitting position – important for keeping airways and the oesophagus open.

✳ Hand-eye-mouth coordination – i.e. your baby can look at something, grab it and bring it to their mouth.

✳ Grown out of the tongue-thrust reflex (called the 'extrusion' reflex) – a protective mechanism whereby your baby automatically pushes food out with their tongue to stop them from choking. They should also be able to move their tongue from side to side.

Around this time your baby will be experiencing various other physical developments that will enable them to deal with solid food. This includes growth of their oral cavity, creating more space for food in the mouth, as well as neuro-muscular coordination, which allows them to munch, chew, swallow or spit out. These new-found oral-motor skills also help with speech development. In fact, the two skills develop in parallel.

WHAT SHOULD I FEED MY BABY AND WHAT SHOULD I AVOID?

It is important to realise that there is almost no right or wrong way to wean a baby and that you will probably do things slightly differently with each baby you have. As long as the food is safe (see First Foods opposite), you can be confident in pursuing whatever seems to work best.

TINY TASTES FIRST

For the first 12 months, breast or formula milk provide almost all the nutrients and calories your baby requires for growth and development, so any additional food is a bonus rather than a necessity. Baby weaning should really be referred to as 'complementary feeding' up until 12 months, so do not get distressed if your baby is a bit slow on their feeding journey. Equally, if your baby loves food, let them go for it – this might mean they start to drop their milk feeds more quickly. It's OK either way!

Tiny tastes count most until they are 12 months. Those babies who are given a wide range of fruits and vegetables to try from 6 months are much more likely to choose healthier food later in childhood[25]. Keep on trying a new food, even if they reject it the first time – it can take 10–15 tastes for them to accept it. Persistence is key.

It's not just the veggies that count. Studies have shown that babies love strong flavours like garlic and suckle for longer on the breast when their mother adds garlic to her food[26]. One of the reasons why I have added herbs and spices to many of my recipes is so that your baby gets exposed to a wide variety of flavours as early on as possible, even if this is only in small amounts.

EXTRAS FOR BREASTFED BABIES

Exclusively breastfed babies will need to start getting some iron from their food from 6 months as breast milk does not contain this important mineral. Iron is added to infant milk formula, so this is less of a concern for bottle-fed babies (but still aim to give a little twice a day if you can by feeding your baby some beef, pulses or eggs). Iron is very important for growth, brain health and immunity; for more information see page 34.

Breast milk is also a very poor source of vitamin D, which is a nutrient critical for immunity, bone strength and mood, so your baby will need to supplement and can also get some from eating eggs and fish, as well as sun exposure. Bottle-fed babies who drink more than 500ml formula daily will be getting just enough vitamin D, but it is also good to top up with foods rich in vitamin D and a little sun. You can learn more about the importance of vitamin D on page 34.

Levels of brain-food nutrients, like zinc[27], choline[28] and omega 3[29], in breast milk are very dependent on the dietary intake of the mother. This is why it is critical for breastfeeding mums to focus on nourishing themselves properly all the way up to their baby's first birthday, while the primary source of nutrition is still breast milk. My recipes have been crafted to feed both mummy and baby, so that you benefit from the right nourishment in unison.

FIRST FOODS – HOW TO START

Even though there are quite a few different approaches on how to start weaning, it's generally thought best to introduce your baby to single vegetables for the first week or so. Many parents start with greens, like broccoli, courgette or green beans, as these introduce your baby to slightly more bitter vegetables first. Don't be afraid to try them on kale either! If they are not introduced early, greens tend to be top of the veg-dodger list later down the line.

The early months are your chance to get in as much variety as possible, as it's thought that the sooner you introduce lots of different tastes and textures, the more likely your child will continue to be a good eater in the longer term. Once you have given the green veg a go, try some root veggies, like butternut squash, carrot, parsnip and swede, and you can also try some steamed and blended apple or pear, raw banana or avocado.

Most parents start with one meal a day and I suggest this is either at breakfast time or mid-morning after a milk feed, so they are not too hungry or fractious. Food allergies are now quite common and if there is an allergic reaction to a food, it may also be easier to get medical care earlier in the day. Allergic reactions usually happen the second time a baby eats a new food, so it is important to try each new food at least twice to be sure it is safe for your little one.

You can build up to two meals quite quickly over the first month, and then take your cue from your baby's hunger levels as to when they are ready for three meals a day, which is usually around the 8- to 9-month mark. Babies under 12 months should not need snacks in between meals as they are still getting milk feeds.

I always suggest offering your baby three types of food texture right from the start – purées, mashed food and hand-held steamed batons of vegetables – you will soon see a pattern in the food that works best for them. Keep on trying all three textures all the way through the first year and beyond, as a baby's food preferences can change all the time. You are aiming for your baby to enjoy a wide range of textures. This will give you a lot more food flexibility going forward, and will give you more options when you are eating outside the home.

BABY PURÉES

Baby purées are the most common way to introduce solids and this is the style of food you will find in pouches and jars in the supermarkets. They are easy for a baby to eat, especially when they don't have any teeth. When preparing them yourself, simply peel and chop your veg into small pieces and steam gently for about 10–12 minutes to get the right lump-free consistency. Blend or mash them with a little breast milk, steamed water or homemade chicken, fish or veg stock (i.e. with no added salt) to make it easy to slip down the throat. You will probably need more liquid than you think, and there is no exact science – the juiciness, dryness and size of food ingredients can vary considerably.

You will probably need 1 cup of liquid to blend 1 whole sweet potato, for example – start with ½ cup, blend for 30 seconds, then add ¼ cup more and blend again, and a further ¼ cup, if needed. You can always add a little bit more liquid and blend again if it's still a bit thick.

Fruit is naturally juicy, and you generally don't need to add liquid to these blends. Banana, avocado, mango and a ripe juicy pear only need to be peeled and do not need to be cooked. Tinned pulses, nut butters and seeds do not need to be cooked before you blend them either.

Once you are able to bring in more complex combinations and flavours, and you have added in a range of ground-up seeds, nut butters, pulses, egg, meat and fish, the rule of thumb is that baby veg purées should be around 40% liquid or fruit, 30% veg and 30% protein, fat and other flavoursome ingredients.

Once your baby has tried each new fruit or veg twice and you know they are not allergic to it, you can start adding tasty twists using herbs and spices, or combine two or three vegetables or fruits together, which is the real start to their taste journey. Add a pinch of herb or spice to a batch of each purée or mash. Use finely chopped fresh herbs, dried or frozen herbs, powdered spices and ground seeds (see pages 24–5).

10 DELICIOUS EARLY FOODS
1. Butternut squash and fennel seeds
2. Sweet potato and rosemary
3. Carrot and cumin
4. Courgette and oregano
5. Pea and mint
6. Broccoli and garlic
7. Kale and coriander
8. Apple and cinnamon
9. Pear and cardamom seeds
10. Mango and nutmeg

Once herbs and spices have been introduced successfully, you can start cooking proper family recipes for you and your baby (see pages 99–171).

SOFT AND MASHED FOOD
Traditionally, weaning guidelines have recommended that soft and mashed foods are introduced from about 10 months, but some young babies get the hang of this texture much earlier and can be very skilled at eating soft, smashed-up food even from 6 months.

Once your baby is through the first phase of trying individual foods, I would encourage you to start making lots of different soft foods that can slip down easily, such as soups, stews, pies, risottos and little pasta dishes. Load the spoon for them and let them try to feed themselves. They might use their hands instead, which is fine!

The mashed food approach is probably the best way to get the most nutrition into your baby and it gives them a lovely sense of independence if they can feed themselves. It's a perfect halfway house between traditional baby feeding and baby-led feeding; it is also very tummy-friendly and optimises flavour and veg intake. And it means you can produce food that the whole family can enjoy. Take, for example, a beef pasta ragu or a fish pie – you just add a little bit more seasoning for older children and adults before serving.

If your baby struggles with the mashed texture to begin with, simply whizz it up in a blender with a little bit more liquid and you have a purée ready for them to try instead, so food is never wasted.

°°°

PERFECT SOFT FOODS FOR BABIES

As well as fruits and vegetables, use the following soft foods in your baby's mashed-up food:

✳ Eggs

✳ White fish – cod, haddock and coley (deboned and skins removed)

✳ Oily fish – salmon, trout, mackerel and sardines (deboned and skins removed)

✳ Seafood – prawns

✳ Poultry – slow-cooked (steamed or poached) chicken, turkey, partridge, guinea fowl and duck. Ideally choose brown meat as it is softer and more nutritious than the breast, which also tends to be drier

✳ Meat – slow-cooked, high-fat-content beef, lamb, pork and venison

✳ Liver – limited to a couple of times a week

✳ Tofu or tempeh soya

✳ Butter and ghee (clarified butter)

✳ Yoghurt, kefir, coconut yoghurt and nut yoghurts

✳ Oat milk, coconut milk and coconut cream

✳ Grated Cheddar, cream cheese, ricotta, mascarpone, cottage cheese and nut cheeses

✳ Grains – brown rice, red rice, black rice, orzo, pearled barley, pearled spelt, couscous, baby pasta shapes and millet

✳ Pseudo-grains – quinoa, buckwheat and amaranth

✳ Pulses – butterbeans, kidney beans, black beans, chickpeas, flageolet beans, cannellini beans, lentils, split yellow peas, as well as legume-based pasta and rice, like red lentils or chickpea pasta and rice

✳ Salt-free nut butters and ground nuts, like ground almonds, peanuts, cashews and hazelnuts, as well as ground macadamia, pecans, pine kernels and walnuts

✳ Seeds – ground sunflower, pumpkin, sesame, chia, flax and hemp, as well as seed butters and tahini

✳ Fresh chicken, lamb, fish or vegetable stock (see pages 204–5 for recipes), steamed vegetable water and very low-salt stock cubes

°°°

TIP: Finger foods tend to be quite slippery, so either cut fruit and veg using a crinkle-cut knife or keep the skin on the bottom third so your baby has something to grip on to. The skin will be spat out, if they reach that far before dropping it! Pull bananas apart with your fingers, rather than cutting them with a knife, as this makes them much easier to grip.

BABY-LED WEANING AND FINGER FOODS

Letting your baby feed themselves has become very popular in recent years – and understandably so. Baby-led weaning is where you put 'finger food', such as steamed veggie batons or small chunks of soft fish, onto your baby's highchair tray, letting them pick up and try things on their own, rather than feeding them puréed or mashed food. Not only does this give your baby some independence right from the start, it also helps with their dexterity and lets them learn that food does not always have a uniform taste or texture. As you can easily integrate family meals with this approach, it is also less time-consuming for parents and your baby feels more included.

However, it is best not to take this approach 100% of the time. Giving your baby mainly hand-held dry foods does not allow maximum nutrition. Furthermore, as this dry food is often served on divided plates, the child can come to expect all foods to be separated from each other. If they are only given hand-held dry food, a child may also shy away from sauces and wet foods in the longer term – and these are a brilliant way of getting in the goodness that they need.

The hand-held-only approach can also cause problems if they go through a fussy eating stage when unwell or teething. That's when the veggies are often ditched for toast or crackers and, before you know it, they are choosing mainly easy-to-eat beige foods, which tend to be carb-heavy and less nutritious. I have therefore included many highly nutritious sweet and savoury hand-held recipes in this book to entice your baby even if they are going through a fussy stage.

In my clinical experience and from weaning my own three babies, an approach that blends all three methods – puréed, mashed and finger foods – is the best way forward. This could look like berry porridge or scrambled egg and soldiers for breakfast, and for lunch and supper a choice of soups, stews, curries, savoury muffins and waffles, with the occasional fruit purée or smoothie bowl for pudding. However, go with the flow, as every single baby is an individual!

FIRST FINGER FOODS

✳ Veggies (steamed in batons or florets): broccoli, cauliflower, kale, carrot, celeriac, sweet potato, white potato, butternut squash, parsnip, asparagus and swede

✳ Fruits that can be given raw: avocado, cucumber, banana, melon, soft pear and mango

✳ Protein: boiled eggs, salmon, white fish, chicken or turkey (baking fish or poultry in parchment paper for 15–20 minutes makes them lovely and soft, but still grabbable)

As with everything when it comes to diet, it is important to strike a balance. Finger foods should definitely be offered to a baby right from the start, ideally from 6 months. Incidentally, when preparing finger foods, they should initially be about the size and shape of an adult finger, to prevent the risk of choking and to allow a better grip. They should also be soft enough to squish between your finger and thumb – this is important in the case of florets of broccoli and cauliflower and batons of root veggies. Remember babies don't need teeth to tackle finger foods, their gums are pretty tough!

HOW DO I KNOW IF MY BABY LIKES A FOOD?

A baby rarely beams with a massive smile when they are first starting to eat solid foods. Sometimes they look excited to be getting some food, but quite a lot of the time they don't look that engaged in the process, and they might even grimace. Don't take that as a cue they dislike the food or are unhappy, it's just their way to show you that they are taking on board new tastes and textures. Keep on going, even if it looks like they are not enjoying it that much! And simply stop feeding them when they start to fuss a bit. Pushing a new food out with their tongue is also pretty normal – although if this happens before or around 6 months it may be a developmental sign that your baby is not quite ready for solid food yet.

CREATING A POSITIVE FEEDING ENVIRONMENT

✳ Overlook the mess – your baby doesn't mind it, but does mind if you get stressed

✳ Feed your baby in the kitchen so they associate this with the place that food happens – the cooking smells also help with their digestion!

✳ Follow their cues

✳ Allow them to play with food

✳ Switch your phone off while feeding – give them 100% of your focus

✳ Use eye contact and engage with your baby

✳ Serve small portions – their tummies are tiny

✳ Make delicious food that you enjoy too

✳ Offer colourful food – try and feed them each colour of the rainbow every day

✳ Remember to smile and have fun

✳ Eat alongside them as a family whenever possible

TIP: Don't force feed or push them for 'one more bite', as this has no benefit and may instil negative associations with eating later on down the line.

FOODS TO AVOID FOR BABIES UNDER 12 MONTHS

These are the foods to avoid or take care with until your baby reaches 12 months. They can be given in small amounts when they are toddlers, but don't go overboard straightaway!

Salt

Babies should only have a tiny amount of salt in their diet (less than 1g salt or 0.4g sodium per day), or they can suffer damage to their kidneys. Since salt is hidden in many foods that your baby is likely to eat, like bread, you should not add salt to any foods that you give them. Also aim to choose foods that are naturally low in salt or have a low-salt or unsalted version. Avoid very salty foods like Marmite, bacon, ham, sausages, smoked salmon, anything in brine, some cheeses (see below) and soya sauce. You should also steer clear of crisps, ready-meals, takeaways and salted chips. Choose unsalted butter, crackers, nut butters, beans and pulses, and very low-salt stock cubes or fresh stock.

Dairy

Babies and young children shouldn't be given unpasteurised milk or cheese as they may carry a nasty bacteria called listeria. This includes mould-ripened soft cheeses, such as brie or camembert and soft blue-veined cheese; although they can be used in cooking, as the heat kills it. Some cheeses also have a substantial amount of salt in them, which may not be shown on the label, so don't go overboard. The worst culprits are cheeses like halloumi, feta and Roquefort. Cottage cheese or cream cheese probably have the least. Your handy Cheddar is OK in moderation.

Sugar

It's best to try to avoid giving any refined white sugar to little ones, mainly because it is not good for their teeth, but also because it provides empty calories with no nutritional benefit. Most of my recipes are sweetened with fruit, the occasional dash of date syrup, coconut sugar or maple syrup.

Honey

Honey is not suitable for babies under 12 months, due to a small risk of infant botulism[30], so avoid it entirely until your baby reaches their first birthday. After that, honey is actually helpful for soothing sore throats and coughs.

Too much rice

The way that rice is grown means that it is naturally exposed to high levels of arsenic, whether it is grown organically or conventionally. This is why the government advises against consuming rice milk during the first year of life, and you should be careful not to give your babies and toddlers too many rice cakes. Many plant 'milks' and gluten-free flours contain high levels of rice, too, so give these sparingly or find rice-free versions. Babies can eat rice with a meal a couple of times a week, but ideally it should be soaked overnight and then washed thoroughly to remove any impurities.

GAGGING AND CHOKING

You should never leave your baby alone whilst eating, and they must always be supported in an upright position. Some babies are like little gerbils and store food in their cheeks at the end of a meal, so always check for this when you bring them down from their highchair, so they don't gag or choke on it later.

It's very important to understand the difference between gagging and choking so that you can keep calm, if it happens to your baby.

Gagging is very common in babies when they are first starting on solids, and it is your baby's safety mechanism. This is how your baby pushes food away from the airway if it is too big to be swallowed. And it is very different from choking, which is when an airway is partially or completely blocked.

Signs of gagging include:

✳ Coughing or retching

✳ Eyes watering

✳ Bringing food back up

Choking is much more serious and if your baby is unable to cry or cough, is silent or struggling to breathe, then you need to perform back blows and chest thrusts as taught on baby first aid courses. I recommend that all new parents go on a baby first aid course so you know exactly what to do. All ages are at risk of choking, but children under 3 years are particularly vulnerable.

To reduce the risk of choking:

✳ Avoid foods that can block airways, such as chunks of food that could be swallowed whole, like cheese, raw apple or raw carrot

✳ Always cut grapes and olives in half

✳ Slice cherry tomatoes into quarters

✳ Squish or cut up large blueberries and butter beans

✳ Remove stones from fruit, such as cherries and peaches

✳ Debone fish thoroughly

✳ Avoid whole nuts

✳ Avoid popcorn

SPICING IT UP

Herbs and spices can be given to babies very early in their weaning journey. This not only adds to the variety of tastes they are exposed to, but also helps to make some foods more palatable – especially when you need to avoid salt and sugar. However, I usually recommend you offer all foods in their natural state first. As a Master Herbalist, I also use herbs and spices in a medicinal way, to soothe little health niggles. They can provide all kinds of natural goodness.

∗ Basil – usually a winning flavour for babies and toddlers, fresh basil leaves make wonderful pesto. See my Pumpkin Seed Pesto on page 121.

∗ Cardamom – has a floral, minty and peppery taste and works well in both sweet and savoury dishes. It is one of our favourites: try adding it to pear, carrot or sweet potato purée, chicken, porridge, rice pudding, muffins or banana bread. Cardamom is settling for the tummy. Try my Raspberry, Sweet Potato & Cardamom Bliss on page 68.

∗ Cinnamon – warm and spicy, this adds delicious flavour to sweet and savoury meals. It is also known to help balance blood sugar levels. Try adding it to apple purée, banana, sweet potato, fruit compote, muffins, waffles, pancakes, porridge and stews. Start the day with my Apple & Cinnamon Overnight Oats on page 78.

∗ Coriander – another tummy-settling aromatic herb, which works beautifully in curries, dhal and chilli, as well as with apple, blueberry and oranges. Roasted Carrot & Tangerine Hummus on page 48 is a perfect early weaning food.

∗ Cumin – has a sweet, nutty, earthy flavour that pairs well with meats, pulses and veg. Try adding it to carrot or cauliflower purée, lamb, chicken, curry and dhal.

∗ Dill – the best herb to use for a sensitive tummy. Mix into avocado, beetroot, cucumber, peas, eggs, potato and smoked fish. The Trout and Dill Pâté on page 55 is delicious and easy.

∗ Fennel – a good settler for windy tummies. Add the seeds to white fish, prawns, tomato sauces and meat dishes. You could also try letting them sip on cooled fennel tea.

∗ Garlic – naturally antifungal, combine it with thyme, rosemary, sage or Eastern spices, like turmeric, cumin and coriander, to give a lovely depth of taste to recipes. It lifts vegetables such as broccoli, cauliflower, potato and tomato. Rosemary & Garlic Chips on page 125 always go down well.

∗ Ginger – one of nature's antibiotics. Add a little ginger powder or grate some fresh root ginger into almond butter, apricot, beef, pork, chicken, butternut squash, cabbage, mango, orange or rhubarb. Munch on the Nut-Free Breakfast Squares on page 79.

✳ Mint – has a lovely fresh taste and is sweet yet cooling. Great for adding to both sweet and savoury purées, like potatoes, tomatoes, carrots and peas, and it adds a fresh kick to fruits like strawberries or mangoes. Minty Pea & Ricotta Dip on page 49 is a winner.

✳ Nutmeg – very popular with babies and has a warming sweet and peppery flavour. It is lovely grated into both sweet baked foods, as well as creamy, savoury dishes. Try adding it to muffins, stewed fruit and white sauces. A hearty breakfast of Coconut & Peach Rice Pudding (see page 67) makes a great start to the day.

✳ Oregano – an Italian herb used in pizza and pasta sauces. Try adding it to veggie purées, roasted vegetables and eggs.

✳ Paprika – has a sweet, rich, smokey taste. It pairs well with sweet potato, carrots, chicken, fish, lentils, paella, chilli and eggs. Try my Appley Baked Beans (see page 96) at breakfast or as a quick lunch.

✳ Parsley – has a lovely fresh and homely taste that adds iron and vitamin C to food. Sprinkle it finely onto potatoes, chicken, fish, fishcakes, carrots and eggs, and add it to juices, smoothies and pesto. Keep it simple with Parsley Couscous (see page 110).

✳ Rosemary – this has a lovely wholesome smell and taste, and you only need a little. It adds aroma and flavour to purées, savoury dishes

and even sweet baked goods. It has been used traditionally to help reduce stress. My Sweet Potato & Rosemary Waffles on page 166 are sublime.

✳ Saffron – a Spanish spice used in paella and Moroccan tagines. This has also been found to help support stress response and to help children focus and concentrate. It peps up any rice dish, and goes well with fish. Fortunately, you only need a little, as it is quite expensive! I have added some to my Brain Box Cookie recipe on page 178.

✳ Sage – naturally antibacterial. Pairs beautifully with anchovy, apple, onion, butternut squash, chicken, egg, liver, pork and tomato. Another herb that helps with focus and memory. Find this combined with chicken liver on page 103.

✳ Thyme – has antimicrobial properties, so it is good to eat this regularly. Add it to chicken, beef, pork, lamb, mushrooms, onions, and tomato. My Celeriac & Apple Mash on page 53 makes a great early weaning food.

✳ Turmeric – a bright yellow, anti-inflammatory spice with countless health properties. It has a mellow taste and a little goes a long way. Try adding it to lentils, eggs, porridge, cauliflower purée, curries and stews, or sprinkled on sweet potato chips (see page 117).

✳ Vanilla – has a natural sweetness and pairs beautifully with apple, apricot, banana, berries, cherries, coconut, fig, hazelnut, peaches and rhubarb. Babies and toddlers love the Frozen Kefir Berry Drops (see page 198).

FUSSY EATING SOS

Every child is a picky eater at some point, and food refusal is very normal. A child's appetite can be unpredictable and almost anything can send it off kilter. If this is happening more than you like, then take a step back, take the pressure off both you and your baby, and try to work out why. In the meantime, it's important to continue offering food three times a day as calmly and straightforwardly as you can, even if the food is rejected and thrown on the floor.

I usually find that picky eating first appears at the time of teething in babies. With toddlers and older children, it can creep in following an illness or a series of minor illnesses, such as a gastric upset or an ear infection. Undiagnosed food sensitivities, low zinc or iron, antibiotic use and ongoing low-grade infections also often feature. In other cases, the child may have developed a fear of a specific food, due to a previous gagging or choking experience.

Physical issues like a high arched palate or enlarged tonsils can hinder chewing and swallowing. And reflux can be an ongoing problem for children of all ages; a cause both of great pain and problems keeping food down. These issues all have the potential to make children very selective eaters or have small appetites. If your child is experiencing any of these problems, please seek professional advice from a paediatric feeding specialist, rather than battling along on your own.

I have confidence in parents' instincts and I always ask mums and dads what *they* think is the root cause of their child's fussy eating. Nine times out of ten, a parent's hunch is spot on and they simply need to have their intuition confirmed. I have given lots of ideas on how to deal with fussy eating in *The Good Stuff*, but here is a summary of those that specifically focus on baby and toddler selective eating.

POST-ILLNESS FOOD REGRESSION

When babies are unwell, they usually stop eating automatically; it's a natural instinct to allow their bodies to heal. This is when they really only need fluids to keep them going. Sometimes in the aftermath of an infection, they become gannets and eat masses, but other times the food refusal lingers, or they will only eat very plain foods, like toast, yoghurt and banana. This is often a sign that they need a little extra zinc to rebuild their immune system and re-ignite their sense of taste and smell. Having enough iron in their bloodstream can also restore the appetite, so if they are pale and pasty, consider this. If they have taken antibiotics, then probiotics, live yoghurt and kefir may help settle the tummy and get their vitality back.

TROUBLE IN THE TUMMY

When there is constipation, loose stools or ongoing reflux, this can throw a child's appetite. So you might see your child eating much better once they have done a poo! Foods that can prompt a sluggish bowel into action are pears, prunes, dates, flax seeds, yoghurt and kefir. When things are looser, try a BRAT diet of bananas, rice, apple purée and toast, as this can help. Note that eggs can be a little binding for some kids.

TEETHING TIPS

Teething can be really hard for some babies and this is where Chamomile & Vanilla Teething Biscuits (see page 174), Frozen Kefir Baby Drops (see page 198) and ice lollies (see page 197) are total saviours. Cucumber sticks are also a winner for teething babies.

Most little ones snap back into eating well once they feel better, so keep up the hard work supporting their sleep patterns, gut function and immunity, and slowly but surely you will get them back on track.

PORTION SIZES

A baby's appetite can change frequently and the amount they can eat varies from meal to meal. It depends on how much milk they drink, their mood, whether they are unwell or teething, and the speed of their metabolism. Almost anything can throw a baby's appetite off: being full, bored, excited, sleepy, too hot, too cold, or whether they are due for a nappy change. Sometimes there is no obvious reason.

It also depends on how efficient they are at digesting and extracting the nutrients from their food. The contents of their nappy will be telling – when you spot undigested food or their poo is the colour of what they have been eating, it may indicate that their digestive tract is struggling. Undigested food is a sign that you need to blend things a bit more until their gut matures and can do a better job. Sweetcorn and raisins are the hardest foods to digest, and you may spot these from time to time, which is perfectly normal.

It's also important not to overload your baby's bowl or plate. Offer a little at a time. The best way to gauge how much your baby should eat is to start with a portion the size of one of their open hands. Increase the portion size as their hands grow. It generally works out as about 5–10 teaspoons at 6 months, 2–4 tablespoons from 7–9 months and 4–6 tablespoons from 9 months upwards.

Remember that lots of food will end up on the floor, over their face or on their bib, so plan to have more to hand than you think they will actually eat.

BABY & TODDLER KITCHEN KIT

KITCHEN ESSENTIALS

* Steamer saucepan, a small saucepan with a steamer basket or baby food maker

* Roasting pan

* Frying pan

* Baking sheet

* Food processor or blender

* Sharp knives, scissors and veg peeler

* Wooden or silicone heat-resistant spatulas, spoons and tongs

* A slotted spatula turner

* Fine cheese grater

* Measuring cups and weighing scales

* A set of measuring spoons

* A rolling pin

* Baking parchment paper

* Freezer-safe storage, BPA-free plastic or Pyrex glass containers

* Ice cube trays

* Freezer bags

* A marker pen or labelling stickers

* Reusable pouches to take food out and about

OPTIONAL

* Mini muffin or doughnut trays

* A ceramic waffle maker

* Lolly moulds

* Cookie cutters

WHAT YOU NEED TO FEED YOUR BABY

* Highchair

* Baby spoons

* Baby bowls

* Sippy water cup

* Large bibs

* Flannels

* Kitchen cloths

* Wipeable mat or oil cloth – for the floor below the highchair to catch dropped food or cutlery

MAKING BABY FOOD PREP A BIT MORE TIME-FRIENDLY

* Use either frozen or fresh fruit and veg

* Batch cook and freeze where possible

* Cook meals that you and your baby can both enjoy together

* To thin the food, use whatever you have available – veg water from steaming, cow's milk, plant-based milk, homemade stock, or very low-salt stock cubes. Avoid using formula as it should not be frozen

TIPS ON HOW TO STORE FOOD

Once cooked, food is generally safe:

* At room temperature for 2 hours

* In the fridge for 3 days (except rice which is 24 hours)

* Frozen for 3 months

TIP: Freeze food as ice cubes or in portions – this gives more storage space and is quicker to defrost. Remember to write the contents and the date it was cooked on the container.

Thaw frozen food overnight in the fridge – although, baked foods like muffins defrost quickly and I leave them to thaw in my bag on the way to the park. Waffles can be toasted from frozen.

'BIG' NUTRITION — NURTURING A FLOURISHING & HEALTHY CHILD

Your child's development depends on three key areas of health that are intertwined and are interdependent – these are the Brain, the Immune system and the Gut (BIG). The first thousand days seems to be the critical window to get this essential BIG nutrition trio functioning well, as that is when your baby's mind, immune-resilience and intestinal health are being primed for the future.

So how do you know when you are getting it right? Well, it is often easier to turn this question on its head and look out for signs that something is wrong. You know when one or all of these are out of sync, for example, when your child gets stuck in a health rut and isn't bouncing back after a couple of weeks.

Signs that this may be happening are very varied and can include your child:

✳ Being grumpy, tired and unreasonable for no reason (although this, of course, accurately describes the terrible twos!)

✳ Being more picky with food and become increasingly selective about what they will eat

✳ Producing nappies that just don't seem right – either they are very bunged up and finding it difficult to pass stools, or they are having regular 'poonamis' or getting sore tummies

✳ Struggling to get to sleep or waking at uncivilised times of the night more frequently

✳ Speech and development slowing up or regressing

✳ Sensory system seeming very delicate

✳ Unable to cope with social situations and seeming very anxious

✳ Having dark circles under their eyes and rough, bumpy or itchy skin

✳ Starting to develop allergies, wheezing and food sensitivities

✳ Having a constant runny nose, cough or sore ears

✳ Dropping down or bouncing up growth percentiles

When you get all three BIG nutrition areas working in harmony, you will generally see a very different and blossoming child. Positive signs are that they are eating a broad range of healthy foods; peeing and pooping regularly and easily; sleeping well most of the time; and developing into a chatty, sociable, little bunny, who is easy company and is curious and quick to learn. A healthy and well-nourished child's eyes will be sparkling, they will have smooth, glowing skin, and will be growing at a healthy rate. A well-balanced child is also free from allergies and generally able to throw off childhood illnesses quickly and easily.

Genetics will predispose your children to some of their health challenges, but even if they have been born with a disability or chronic health condition, then all is by no means lost. A child's diet, lifestyle and environment can make a massive difference to their outcomes, and we see cases again and again in our NatureDoc clinics where children develop and thrive better than expected, despite their disability, to become the best versions of themselves.

In reality, children's health tends to yo-yo and it can be hard to get all three elements aligned at once. Like everyone else, kids have good days and bad days, and they can be very unpredictable with their food choices. Don't beat yourself up if they have a day or two eating very little or rubbish, as this is perfectly normal. Just take each day at a time and celebrate the little gains, rather than aiming too high. It's all about building healthy habits, rather than instant perfection. Even the fussiest eaters will get there in the end, although it can sometimes seem like a marathon.

FEEDING THE BRAIN

Omega 3

Omega 3 from oily fish is one of the most important nutrients for a baby's brain. Mothers who eat a diet rich in omega 3, or take fish oil supplements during pregnancy, will be giving their baby a great start to life and it is now also recommended during breastfeeding. Some studies have shown that optimising omega 3 during pregnancy and after birth may also help to prevent postnatal depression.[31, 32, 33]

There are three main forms of omega 3 fatty acids that are important for human development: DHA, EPA and ALA. During the rapid growth of your baby's first year of life, omega 3 in the form of DHA (Docosahexaenoic Acid) is the main one to focus on, as it is needed to develop strong eyes, nerve tissue and a healthy brain[34]. Toddlers also benefit from plenty of DHA, which is known to affect cognition and can have a positive effect on temperament[35] and help a young child emotionally regulate themselves.

To get enough DHA, ideally your little one should eat oily fish, such as salmon, mackerel, trout or sardines 2–3 times per week. Try my Eggy Salmon & Dill Muffins (see page 94) or Trout & Dill Pâté (see page 55). There is some omega 3 in walnuts, chia and flax seeds, but research has found that the type of omega 3 in these (ALA) does not convert easily into the DHA form[36], so if your child does not eat enough oily fish, or you are a vegetarian or vegan household, then you need to eat these secondary sources much more frequently or take a fish-based or vegan omega 3 supplement.

Iodine

Pregnant and breastfeeding mums need to consume plenty of iodine for their baby's brain to develop normally. Iodine-deficient women have been found to have children with significantly lower scores of verbal IQ and lower reading ability[37]. Iodine also feeds the thyroid, which is important for a healthy and efficient metabolism and it's important for the immune system.

Formula milk contains the requisite amount of iodine for a baby, while breastfed children are dependent on the iodine stores in their mother's diet. Either way, I encourage introducing iodine-rich foods nice and early in the weaning process. Babies with cow's milk protein allergy tend to have lower levels of iodine, whether they are formula- or breastfed, so this is a key nutrient to remember for these babies[38].

Fish is a great way to give your child iodine and cod contains the most. Try my Fish Pie with Cheesy Potato & Broccoli Mash (see page 107) or Pesto Fish Bites (see page 148).

Seaweed is a very concentrated and flavourful source of iodine and your children can either munch on the odd nori seaweed strip or you can add seaweed flakes or granules to their food instead. You can over-do iodine, so be careful of some types of seaweed, which contain a lot more than you need.

Seafood and dairy products also contain good levels, and prunes, bananas and peas contain a little bit. People who live by the sea even benefit from the iodine in the sea air. Iodine is now added to some plant-based 'milks' often labelled 'potassium iodide'. A young child needs 90mcg iodine daily[39] to keep their levels up, which is about a third of a fillet of cod. There is 14mcg in a salmon steak.

Folate and vitamin B12
Folate and B12 work together to nourish a baby, prevent neural tube defects and to enable brain development. If a child doesn't get enough B12 in their diet, it can affect folate levels and vice-versa. These are critical for red blood cell production, for optimal brain and neurological function, as well as helping digestion and improving iron uptake. This is why kids need to eat their greens! Natural folate is found in leafy greens, like kale, spinach and broccoli, as well as in beetroot, avocado, asparagus and pulses, such as chickpeas and lentils. Vitamin B12 is found in meat, fish and eggs. Ideally you would consume folate- and B12-rich foods together – this may explain why a plate of 'meat and two veg' has evolved over time. Try my Beefy Quinoa & Beetroot Burgers (see page 135).

Those babies with the lowest levels of B12 are generally exclusively breastfed by mothers who have followed a vegan or vegetarian diet, and supplementation is very important for these mums and babies. Marmite and nutritional yeast do contain a little, but most vegans rely on B12 supplements. Babies need a minimum of 0.4–0.5mcg daily, toddlers 0.9mcg daily and school-age kids between 1.2mcg and 1.8mcg. There are no upper limits for B12 consumption[40].

Choline
Choline is another B vitamin critical for your baby's brain development[41]. It plays an important role in learning and building a good memory[42], as well as attention and problem solving[43] and to

prevent anxiety[44]. It is just as important as folate for protecting a baby from birth defects – indeed they work in harmony. Our babies need a constant supply, both in utero and in their diet after birth. Premature babies or those born with a low birth weight need more choline than babies who reach full term[45]. Unfortunately, most prenatal multivitamins do not contain choline[46], so the role of diet is critically important.

Choline-rich foods include liver, eggs, meat, sunflower seeds, peanut butter, tofu, beetroot and spinach. Try my Sage & Cranberry Chicken Liver Pâté (see page 103) or Mini Avocado, Carrot & Blueberry Muffins (see page 184). Babies need at least 125–150mg per day of choline and toddlers a little more at 200–250mg per day[47]. There is around 147mg in one large egg.

FEEDING THE IMMUNE SYSTEM

We have all become increasingly aware in recent times of the importance of immunity. The Coronavirus pandemic has shown us that the same virus can affect people very differently in terms of severity and symptoms, and evidence is mounting that a person's underlying conditions, nutrition and metabolic health are crucial factors in determining the duration and degree of a viral or bacterial infection.

Much of our immune status is effectively laid down during our early childhood, which is why it is so important to get babies' and toddlers' diets right. The early years are when

some core nutrients are needed to form a healthy immune response both in the short and long term.

Having a healthy immune system is not just about dodging colds, coughs and sniffles. The system can also misfire and trigger autoimmune conditions, such as type 1 diabetes, juvenile idiopathic arthritis, inflammatory bowel or coeliac disease. And it can become overzealous and reactive, manifesting in allergies. Diet can do a great deal both to ensure that these problems do not set in and to help rebalance a wayward immune system, in order that any symptoms can be managed more easily. There are some key nutrients that help and these include vitamin C, vitamin D, zinc and iron. However, these are not standalone nutrients and the immune system's complex needs must be fed with a varied and nutritious diet.

Vitamin C

Vitamin C is vital for immunity and can be taken to prevent or treat upper respiratory infections. Incidentally, vitamin C cannot reduce the severity of a common cold, but it can reduce its duration[48]. Foods need to be eaten in their raw state to bestow the greatest benefits of vitamin C – this is why I tend to add things like lemon juice and parsley to foods before serving. As well as oranges, lemons and limes, good sources of vitamin C are strawberries, pineapple and especially kiwi fruit. It can also be found in red peppers and kale. Try the Coconut Yoghurt & Lime Dip (see page 56) or the Lemon & Blueberry Smoothie Bowl (see page 61).

Vitamin D

Why does sunshine make us feel so good? It's because we need it to create vitamin D, which is vital for every single cell and function in our body. A vitamin D deficiency is one of the principal causes of weakened bendy bones, known as rickets[49], and tooth decay in children. It's also linked to a poor immune system and even low mood. Optimal vitamin D levels seem to be particularly important for those with learning and neuro-developmental difficulties[50]. The lack of sunshine in the UK, particularly in the winter months, is a major reason why we tend to fall short. Added to which, parents now tend to slap on sun cream as soon as the sun comes out, which blocks the rays which promote vitamin D production. It's now thought that letting your child have a few minutes of sun, cream-free, before application, makes all the difference to their vitamin D levels[51]. As everyone's skin differs in sensitivity, be sure to keep your child sun-safe and ensure their skin does not burn.

A number of foods contain vitamin D, including red meat, eggs and oily fish, which is the best source. Try Mini Sardine & Sweetcorn Quiches (see page 144) or Salmon Couscous Burgers (see page 149).

However, we are now all advised to top up our levels of vitamin D during the winter with supplements, as our diet tends not to provide enough. Children from birth to four should have at least 10mcg supplement daily (400iu)[52]. Babies who drink more than 500ml baby milk formula daily usually do not need any additional vitamin D.

Zinc

Zinc is an essential nutrient for immunity, proper growth and brain development[53], so this is an important mineral to get right throughout childhood. When kids have a growth-spurt, they can dip in zinc, so may need more during these times. A zinc deficiency can be one of the reasons for a poor appetite[54], as it helps to fire up our gastric juices. Low zinc stores can alter our sense of taste and smell[55], and may be why a child becomes pickier with their food after illness. Zinc-rich foods include eggs, salmon, prawns, milk, chickpeas, peas, dates and pumpkin seeds. Try my Butternut Squash & Kale Mac 'n' Cheese (see page 162) or Asian Prawn Fried Rice (see page 141).

Iron

Low iron levels are common in little children, especially if they do not eat much red meat[56] or green veg[57]. Toddlers who drink too much cow's milk[58] are also at higher risk of developing low iron levels, known as anaemia (milk can block the absorption). Premature babies may also need a little bit more.

Iron is an essential nutrient for growth[59], immunity[60] and to enable children to think properly[61]. Iron helps to transport oxygen in the blood around the body and brain. There are many signs of iron deficiency and these can include poor appetite, as well as pale skin, tiredness, general weakness, headaches, shortness of breath, dizziness, hair loss, tongue swelling, tingling in the legs and slow growth rate.

Babies and toddlers should ideally consume iron twice a day and foods with iron include red meat, liver, eggs, spinach, broccoli, lentils, chickpeas, kidney and black beans, sesame seeds, apricots and molasses. According to the BDA, babies of 7–12 months need 7.8mg iron daily and toddlers need 6.9mg[62], which is a huge amount considering 1 large egg contains 1.1mg, 100g broccoli 1mg and 100g kidney beans or chickpeas 2mg. Milk formula does provide a little iron, so bottle-fed babies are less dependent on iron in their diet than breastfed babies. Vitamin C helps iron absorption, so always try and give your baby fruit with an iron-rich meal. The ultimate iron boost is my Sage & Cranberry Chicken Liver Pâté (see page 103), or you can try Supercharged Beef & Lentil Ragu with Spaghetti (see page 126). For plant-based families, try the Carrot & Apricot Falafels on page 151 or Mexican Black Bean Pâté on page 50.

FEEDING GUT FLORA

We all have billions of magical microbes living in our digestive tract. Think of these microbes as a glorious and diverse community of helpers that are fuelled by the healthy, natural foods we eat. Each person's gut eco-system is unique and is changing all the time. It helps to control everything from our mood to our learning potential and our immunity. The gut microbiome is such an important topic that over 15,000 scientific papers were published on it in 2019 alone.

In the few weeks leading up to birth, amazing changes occur in the mother, whereby the dendritic cells in her gut lining migrate to the tissue at the back of her breasts, forming a channel so that her gut flora can pass into her breast milk[63, 64]. It is this mechanism that feeds the baby with the beneficial bacteria which it needs to build a healthy immune system and to develop well. And is one of the reasons breastfeeding is encouraged. It's also why a healthy diet is so important for a breastfeeding mum, as her microbiome will be reflected in the baby's gut flora.

Some milk formulas do contain prebiotic and probiotic strains to encourage the gut flora to proliferate, but they will never be as diverse as those from breast milk. You can also give babies probiotic supplements from birth. These are particularly beneficial if mum or baby have needed antibiotics or are on reflux medication, as these are both known to reduce the gut diversity considerably. Early antibiotic use can sensitise the baby to their environment and it is thought to be part of the complex picture behind allergies[65], asthma[66] and eczema[67]. A baby's weaning stage is the first proper chance for a fully bottle-fed baby to start building up a diverse range of gut flora, and thus benefit from these microbes, which can reduce allergy risk, build a bright, happy, switched-on brain and help the child to develop a robust immune system.

Here are the ways that you can help your little one to build a healthy gut microbiome:

Feed the rainbow

Why are fruits and vegetables so vital? One of the main reasons is that they contain important microbiome-boosting antioxidants known as polyphenols. These are the brightly coloured, naturally occurring pigments found in many vegetables and fruit – think red in raspberries, tomatoes, cranberries and red apples; orange in satsumas, apricots, carrots and sweet potato; yellow in mango, lemons, bananas and yellow peppers; green in broccoli, kiwi fruit, peas and courgettes; and purple in plums, red grapes, blueberries and blackberries. This is a time of life when babies are particularly attracted to bright colours, so take full advantage. Try my Smokey Prawn & Pea Paella (see page 143) or Zingy Hummus Trio (see pages 47–8) to introduce the rainbow foods to your family.

Adopt a Mediterranean diet

The diversity and fresh ingredients in a Mediterranean diet offer one of the best ways to bolster the microbiome and reduce systemic inflammation. This is why my recipes are rich in vegetables, fruits, pulses, nuts, seeds, oily fish, meat, olive oil, fresh herbs and wholegrains.

Eat fermented foods

Full-fat natural live yoghurt and kefir are two wonderful cultured foods that help to restore a healthy microbiome. One of the main types of bacteria they contain is lactobacillus, which helps us digest dairy products and to prime the immune system. Lactobacillus is also one of the building blocks for making acetylcholine, which helps children to learn, process information and build a good memory. On top of this, it makes GABA (Gamma-Aminobutyric Acid), which keeps us calm and relaxed – think of GABA as our inner yogi. Try my Happy Tummy Blueberry Kefir (see page 170).

For babies who are dairy-free or being raised vegan, you can now buy coconut-milk-based kefir and yoghurts, as well as dairy-free probiotics and kefir supplements, which can be popped into a fruit purée or smoothie.

Get outside

Opening your windows, spending time in the garden, or walking and playing in nature are some of the best ways to expose your baby to the natural diversity of microbes in the environment. This is partly why outdoor kids who are allowed to get muddy tend to have better immune systems. Don't be overzealous with antibacterial household cleaning products either, as these can give the microbiome a knocking and lead to more wheezing and asthma down the line[68, 69].

HOW TO FEED A CHILD WITH FOOD ALLERGIES

Crying incessantly, itchy rashes, sore tummies, wheezing, vomiting, diarrhoea, constipation and even toddler behavioural issues are common signs of food allergies. Food allergies now affect almost one in 10 children[70] and the main food allergens that younger kids tend to react to include: eggs, cow's milk, soya, nuts and fish – all foods that are important for a nutritious and balanced diet.

Fortunately, after a few years and a period of dietary exclusion, a child usually grows out of cow's milk, soya, egg and wheat allergies. However, fish, shellfish, peanut and tree nut allergies tend to be life-long and rarely resolve.

An allergy tends to appear in the first two years of life[71] and an allergic reaction is usually only apparent after the child comes into contact with the allergen for a second time[72]. This is why you should expose your child to a food at least twice on its own when weaning them before you know it is safe for them. A child can be allergic to any food that contains protein molecules, so about the only food they cannot be allergic to is sugar!

Bananas, avocados, tomatoes and strawberries are another group of fairly common triggers, which can cause a red rash around the mouth or an itchy mouth or throat in babies; however, severe allergies to these foods are quite rare. Reactions to these are usually due to the naturally occurring histamine in the food and children can often eat a little without any problem.

Various theories have attempted to explain the rise in food allergies and other atopic diseases, such as eczema and asthma, over the last three decades, from the timing and route of introduction of foods into the diet to genetics. Pregnancy is a good place to start if you are hoping to prevent atopic issues in your offspring. It is now known that a higher maternal intake of peanut, milk and wheat during early pregnancy is associated with reduced odds of mid-childhood allergy and asthma[73]. Conversely, too much sugar when pregnant can put your child at greater risk for allergies and asthma[74]. On a positive note, probiotics taken by pregnant women or breastfeeding mothers and/or given to infants appear to reduce the risk of eczema in infants[75].

Other risk factors for developing an allergy may include passive smoking and our clean 'Western lifestyle'[76]. Since kids brought up on farms are less likely to develop asthma and allergies[77], and there is a link between vitamin D deficiency[78] and allergies, I suspect that fresh air, mud and sunshine play a key preventive role.

DAIRY-FREE TIPS

Here are some of the key nutrients that dairy-free kids will need to compensate for in other parts of their diet:

Calcium

A baby needs 525mg per day and they usually get enough via breast milk or hypoallergenic milk formula. A young toddler needs less, at about 350mg calcium daily, which is roughly equivalent to 300ml fortified plant-based milk or 600ml unfortified oat milk. Other sources of dietary calcium include oats, chia seeds, poppy seeds, sesame seeds, almond butter, tahini, tinned salmon, tinned sardines, green leafy veg and oranges, so get your child introduced to these foods when they are babies in order that they are incorporated into their meals going forward. Try Tahini, Mustard & Tarragon Chicken Thighs (see page 122) or Brainy Bliss Balls (see page 188).

Vitamin D

The best sources of Vitamin D, other than sunlight, are fatty animal food products, such as oily fish and egg yolk. This is why eggs and oily fish, such as salmon and sardines, are extra important if a child is on a dairy-free diet (one piece of baked salmon contains around 240iu vitamin D). Vitamin D is added to many fortified milk alternatives; however, it is usually in the plant-based vitamin D2 form, which is less effective than animal-sourced vitamin D3, which is synthesised from sunlight exposure.

Omega 3

Non-dairy 'milk' manufacturers don't fortify their products with omega 3 yet, and it's harder to convert plant-based ALA omega-3 – found in walnuts, chia seeds, flax seeds and hemp seeds – into the brain-building DHA form. So, for dairy-free kids, salmon and oily fish come to the rescue again – one whole 150g salmon steak gives 1,900mg of EPA and DHA omega 3. Babies and toddlers only need to eat one salmon steak spread over a week to get enough.

Iodine

Iodine is essential for healthy thyroid function, which controls our metabolism, growth and learning. Kids need about 90–130mcg per day, depending on their age. White and oily fish contain iodine, as does seaweed, so consider giving your toddler nori sheets to munch on from time to time. Cod is my go-to iodine source; try my Salmon & Cod Potato Fish Cakes (see page 147).

Unfortunately, there is no like-for-like plant-based 'milk' equivalent to dairy milks yet, so if your child is dairy-free, you will need to take their entire diet into consideration to ensure they get all the nutrition they need.

NB You should never replace breast milk or formula with dairy-free alternatives for babies under 12 months. Toddlers over 12 months can drink dairy-free alternatives and oat milk is usually the best choice.

EGG ALLERGIES

Egg allergies are particularly common in kids with eczema, and since eggs are such a powerhouse of nutrition you need to work hard to find other foods to fill the nutrition gap.

The brain food choline in eggs can also be found in sunflower seeds, liver and meat. Vitamin A can be found in yellow butter and mango, as well as orange vegetables, like carrots, butternut squash and sweet potato. Vitamin D can be found in oily fish and organic milk, as well as from the sun in the summer months; while folic acid can be found in green leafy veggies, like spinach, kale as well as broccoli. Egg-free kids do not need to miss out on vitamin B12, as this is also in dairy products, meat, nutritional yeast flakes and Marmite. And to ensure they gain enough iron, choose liver, meat, pulses, spinach, apricots and molasses.

NUT-FREE KIDS

If a nut allergy is found in a child, then often doctors recommend that they avoid all nuts and seeds, which can limit the diet somewhat. Pushing for more in-depth allergy tests will give you a clearer idea as to which nuts and seeds your child is allergic to and which are safe for them to eat. However, sometimes different nuts are handled in the same factory, so if your child is very overreactive to one type of nut they may need to avoid them all anyway.

A child can get all the nutrition they need from their diet without eating nuts; although it is important to compensate for the lack of nuts with other sources of protein, such as meat, fish, eggs, tofu and pulses. If they are not allergic to seeds, then sunflower, pumpkin, sesame, chia, flax and hemp seeds can also be used to boost their healthy fats and omega 3s.

WHAT PLANT-BASED FAMILIES NEED TO KNOW

With the rapid increase of people turning to a vegetarian or wholly vegan diet, and a general trend to reducing our consumption of animal products, I am asked more and more these days about how to provide a nutritious plant-based diet from bump to birth and all the way through childhood[79]. There is a general consensus that a child can be raised on a wholly plant-based diet, but it involves a lot of hard work on the cooking front. This is because most convenience plant-based foods are not that nutritious and are often ultra-processed – it's very hard to make nutritious vegan food with a good shelf-life that has a good texture and taste as well. Home-cooked plant-based food, however, is a whole different story: it can be much more nutritious and, with a little help from some fortified foods and food supplements, can mean your child gets every nutrient they need.

Here are my guidelines to ensure your child gets a nourishing and healthy plant-based diet:

✳ Feed them large amounts and a wide variety of plant foods. These should be whole foods or minimally processed but don't go overboard with fibre when they are tiny, as this can fill them up too quickly – it is a good idea to peel veggies such as carrots and fruit such as apples until their tummies are bigger.

✳ Focus on plant-based sources of omega 3 fatty acids (walnuts, chia seeds, flax seeds, hemp seeds) and top up with marine-algae-based DHA supplements. Aim to give plenty of monosaturated oils (olive oil, extra-virgin rapeseed oil, avocados, avocado oil, most nut and nut oils, sesame seeds, sesame oil, sunflower seeds and organic sunflower oil) while avoiding trans fats (found in fast food), hydrogenated fats (found in shop-bought biscuits, cakes etc, margarine and deep-fried foods) and too many tropical oils (coconut, palm and palm kernel oils). This will help to optimise the efficiency of the omega 3 metabolic pathway, which is important for eye and brain development, as well as for controlling inflammation. A baby or toddler does not need to limit their healthy fats, so give them plenty.

✳ Feed them enough calcium for healthy bones. Oats, chia seeds, tahini and almond butter should become regulars and top up with oat milk, as per my recommendation for dairy-free kids on page 39.

✳ Vitamin D is important for the bones, too, so make sure they get some sunshine and give them vitamin D supplements or foods fortified with vitamin D (see page 34).

✳ Feed them plenty of B vitamins – these include choline, folate and vitamin B12 (see page 32). It is advisable to take a supplement for B12, as this is found primarily in animal-sourced foods and is generally not present in plant foods. Plant-based choline foods include peanut butter, tofu, sunflower seeds, beetroot and spinach.

✳ Bolster their iron. Your kids are going to need to love wholemeal bread, lentils, pulses, molasses and apricots, as well as their greens, or they will have to rely on fortified cereals to get enough iron. Also remember to feed children plenty of vitamin C from oranges, lemons, red peppers and kiwi fruit to help them absorb the iron in their food.

✳ Optimise zinc – grains, legumes, soya, nuts and seeds are good plant sources of this. However, zinc absorption may be impaired by the natural phytate and fibre content of these foods, which is why it is important to soak, sprout and ferment grains and pulses, as well as to peel fruits and veggies for babies. Zinc-optimising foods include sourdough bread, as well as sprouted nuts, seeds and pulses that are now easily found in health food shops. Nutritional yeast is a good source of zinc and its consumption is popular among vegans. Boost a meal with vitamin C to help zinc absorption.

✳ Make sure they get enough protein! This is probably one of the biggest challenges of following a plant-based diet, so parents need to get really savvy with good-quality natural protein sources, including pulses, tofu, tempeh, soya yoghurt, edamame beans, nut butters, tahini, sesame seeds, sunflower seeds, pumpkin seeds, quinoa, buckwheat, chia seeds, hemp seeds and peas. There are also small amounts in wholemeal bread, mulberries, goji berries, jackfruit and vegetables.

To ensure your baby is getting all the essential amino acids from plant proteins they need, you should vary the types of plant protein they eat at every meal. Pseudo-cereals, such as buckwheat, quinoa, amaranth, as well as hemp seeds, provide all the essential amino acids in similar proportions to that of animal protein. Other plant-based protein options, however, need to be combined and this means eating lentils or dhal with wild rice, and chickpeas or peas with quinoa. You can also add a little plant-based protein powder to smoothies or porridge, or to muffin, pancake and waffle mixes, if you feel they are not getting enough. From 6–12 months, breast or formula milk are still good sources of protein in addition to the solid food that is introduced.

CHAPTER ONE

SAVOURY WEANING FOODS

Baby friendly and suitable from the first few weeks of weaning, these recipes can all be turned into dips, spreads or mash for older kids and side dishes for parents – you might want to add a pinch of fine sea salt and a little extra spice for those over 12 months.

SWEET POTATO & BEETROOT

PEA & TURMERIC

ROASTED CARROT & TANGERINE

ZINGY HUMMUS TRIO

These tasty, brightly coloured dips make excellent first foods and they are a great way of introducing complex flavours and getting veggies into little ones. Your baby can eat these straight off a spoon, with veg sticks (steamed until soft) or slathered on crackers or toast.

SWEET POTATO & BEETROOT

Beetroot is full of iron, an important mineral for babies and growing children, while the vitamin A found in sweet potato promotes eye and gut health, as well as general immunity.

SERVES 1–2 CHILDREN
¼ medium sweet potato, peeled and cut into
    4–5cm chunks
1 small beetroot, cooked without vinegar
50g/¼ cup tinned chickpeas, rinsed and drained
1 tsp light tahini paste
½ tsp ground cumin
Squeeze of fresh lime juice
¼ garlic clove, finely chopped
2–3 tbsp olive or cold-pressed rapeseed oil
Freshly ground black pepper (optional)

Steam the sweet potato for 10–15 minutes or until soft. (You can also use leftover baked or mashed sweet potato.)

Place all the ingredients except the oil in a food processor and whizz for a minute until everything is combined.

While the machine is still running, add the oil 1 tablespoon at a time until you get your desired consistency. You can add 1–2 tablespoons water, if you want it smoother.

SESAME-FREE
Swap tahini paste
for 1 tsp cream cheese
or sunflower seed
butter, or leave out.

PEA & TURMERIC

Turmeric is a bright yellow spice that is known for its anti-inflammatory properties. The pulses provide protein and fibre, as well as a good dose of the essential minerals magnesium, potassium and calcium.

SERVES 1 ADULT & 1 CHILD
50g/¼ cup frozen peas
50g/¼ cup tinned cannellini beans,
    rinsed and drained
¼ tsp ground turmeric
Squeeze of fresh lemon juice
1 tbsp avocado oil or olive oil
Freshly ground black pepper (optional)

Place all the ingredients except the oil in a food processor and whizz for a minute until everything is combined.

While the machine is still running, add the oil. You can add 1–2 tablespoons water, if you want it smoother.

 STORAGE

Can be stored in a sealed container in the fridge for 3 days, or in the freezer for up to 3 months.

ROASTED CARROT & TANGERINE HUMMUS

A lovely sweet hummus that's rich in vitamins A, C and K. Serve as a baby purée or encourage your little one to dip broccoli and green beans into it. It's also great spread on Nutty Sweet Potato Toasts (see page 191) and Kefir Flatbreads (see page 132). If you are short of time, you can steam the carrots instead. The hummus will still be good, but roasting carrots really brings out the flavour and is worth the extra effort.

SERVES 1-2 CHILDREN

1–2 carrots, peeled and cut into 2cm cubes
3–4 tbsp olive or cold-pressed rapeseed oil
100g/½ cup tinned chickpeas, rinsed and drained
Juice of 1 tangerine
1 tsp light tahini paste
1 tbsp fresh coriander or mint leaves
Freshly ground black pepper (optional)

Preheat the oven to 180°C/160°C fan/gas mark 4.

Place the carrots on a baking tray and drizzle with 1 tablespoon oil. Season with ground black pepper, if using, and roast for 20–25 minutes, or until tender and lightly golden. Turn the carrots halfway through to ensure they are golden on both sides.

Blend the roasted carrots, chickpeas, tangerine juice, tahini paste and herbs in a food processor. While the machine is still running, add the remaining oil 1 tablespoon at a time until you get your desired consistency. You can add more oil or water, if you want a smoother dip.

STORAGE

Can be stored in a sealed container in the fridge for 3 days, or in the freezer for up to 3 months.

6 MONTHS PLUS

SESAME-FREE
Swap tahini paste for 1 tsp sunflower seed butter, or leave out.

MINTY PEA & RICOTTA DIP

A delicious first food that you can give directly off a spoon. Cream cheese, kefir, yoghurt or cottage cheese are good alternatives to ricotta.

SERVES 1–2 CHILDREN

40g/¼ cup frozen peas
125g/½ cup ricotta
Small sprig of mint,
    leaves finely chopped,
    or 1 tsp dried

STORAGE

Can be stored in a sealed container in the fridge for 3 days, or in the freezer for up to 3 months.

6 MONTHS PLUS

Place the peas in a bowl and pour some boiling water over the top to defrost them.

Drain the peas and place in a food processor with the ricotta and mint. Pulse for about 10 seconds to make a chunky spread or dip for toddlers, or for 1 minute to make a smooth baby purée.

DAIRY-FREE
Use 150g silken tofu or butterbeans instead of ricotta.

MEXICAN DOUBLE

FIRST GUACAMOLE

This recipe works well as a stand-alone baby meal, a dip with crunchy veg or a topping for chilli, quesadillas or tortilla chips. Keep it chunky for older kids and blend it smooth for tinies.

SERVES 1–2 CHILDREN

1 avocado, peeled, stoned and mashed
3 cherry tomatoes, quartered (optional)
30g/¼ cup tinned or frozen sweetcorn, defrosted, if necessary, and drained
Small handful of fresh coriander leaves, finely chopped
Squeeze of fresh lime juice
Freshly ground black pepper (optional)
Few chilli flakes (for adults and older kids only)

Place all the ingredients in a bowl and mix together well. Serve as it is or pop everything in a food processor and whizz for 1 minute for young babies.

Can be stored in a sealed container in the fridge for a few hours. Not suitable for freezing.

BLACK BEAN PÂTÉ

The perfect iron boost for babies and young kids. Delicious on crackers or Nutty Sweet Potato Toasts (see page 191) or as a side dish for a Mexican meal.

SERVES 2–3 CHILDREN

1 × 400g tin black beans, rinsed and drained
Handful of baby spinach leaves, shredded
4 dried apricots (ideally unsulphured), finely chopped
1 tsp treacle or blackstrap molasses
½ tsp ground cumin
1 tbsp water
Few chilli flakes (for adults and older kids only)
Pinch of fine sea salt (not for children under 12 months)

Place all the ingredients in a saucepan over a medium heat and cook for 5–7 minutes, or until soft.

Serve as it is or whizz to a purée for young babies.

Can be stored in a sealed container in the fridge for 3 days, or in the freezer for up to 3 months.

COMFORTING BUTTERNUT & CHESTNUT PURÉE

If you have a packet of chestnuts left over after Christmas, this is a great
way to use them up. Combined with butternut squash and apple,
they make a comforting wintry purée that is naturally sweet.

SERVES 2-3 CHILDREN

½ small butternut squash,
   peeled and diced
1 apple, peeled, cored
   and diced
Knob of unsalted butter
3 whole roasted chestnuts
   or 1 heaped tbsp
   chestnut purée
Sprig of thyme
60ml/¼ cup chicken
   or vegetable stock
   (homemade or very
   low salt)
Freshly ground black
   pepper (optional)
Pinch of fine sea salt
   (not for children
   under 12 months)

Place all the ingredients in a medium saucepan, cover
with a lid and bring to the boil. Reduce the heat and
simmer for 15 minutes, or until the squash is soft.

Remove and discard the thyme sprig. Place the remaining
ingredients in a food processor and whizz to a smooth purée.

Serve the purée on its own, or as a side with your
Sunday roast.

DAIRY-FREE
Use 1 tsp olive oil
instead of butter.

NUT-FREE
Swap the chestnuts
for 1 tbsp pumpkin
seeds and add just
before puréeing.

STORAGE

Can be stored in a sealed
container in the fridge for
3 days, or in the freezer
for up to 3 months.

6
MONTHS
PLUS

MASH IT UP

CELERIAC & APPLE MASH

Mash is an easy way of getting root veggies into reluctant kids as you can disguise the flavour with fruit and herbs. Babies will love this thyme and apple combo as a purée. You could also serve it with sausages or roast chicken for older children or adults.

SERVES 2–3 CHILDREN
½ celeriac, peeled and cubed
1 apple, peeled, cored and grated
100g tinned butterbeans, rinsed and drained
Sprig of thyme or 2 tsp dried
Knob of unsalted butter
Splash of water
Freshly ground black pepper (optional)
Pinch of fine sea salt
   (not for children under 12 months)

Place all the ingredients in a medium saucepan and cover with a lid. Cook over a medium heat for 15 minutes, or until the celeriac is soft.

Remove the thyme sprig and mash the veg, or blitz it in a food processor to a purée.

DAIRY-FREE
Use 1 tsp olive oil
instead of butter.

ROOT VEGGIE MASH

Three veggies in one mash, which can also be puréed for young babies. It makes a great topping for cottage pie or side dish for your Sunday roast.

SERVES 2–3 CHILDREN
1 large white potato, peeled and cut into chunks
¼ swede, peeled and cut into chunks
2 carrots, peeled and cut into chunks
1 tbsp unsalted butter
Freshly ground black pepper (optional)
Pinch of fine sea salt
   (not for children under 12 months)

Place the potato, swede and carrots in a medium saucepan. Cover with water and bring to the boil. Reduce the heat and simmer for 10–15 minutes, or until soft.

Drain the veg and tip back into the pan. Add the butter and seasoning, if using, and mash, or blitz in a food processor with 120ml/½ cup hot chicken or vegetable stock (homemade or very low salt) for a baby purée.

DAIRY-FREE
Use 1 tbsp olive oil
instead of butter.

TROUT & DILL PÂTÉ

Trout is a mild-tasting fish that is bursting with omega 3 fatty acids, which are so important for brain development. Choose smoked trout to make a speedy pâté or fresh trout for a baby under 12 months. Spread it on toast or crackers or serve as a filling for baked potatoes. You could also blend it with some defrosted frozen peas to make a baby purée.

SERVES 3-4 CHILDREN

125g smoked trout or
   1 small fresh trout fillet
50g/¼ cup cream cheese
Juice of ½ lemon
1 tbsp fresh dill,
   finely chopped
Freshly ground black
   pepper (optional)

If using fresh trout, poach the fillet in a little water for 5–7 minutes, or until cooked through. Remove the skin and pick out any bones carefully.

For a smooth pâté, blitz the trout with the other ingredients in a food processor. For a chunkier texture, simply mix it all together with a fork in a bowl.

STORAGE

Can be stored in a sealed container in the fridge for up to 3 days, or in the freezer for up to 3 months.

DAIRY-FREE
Use an oat crème fraîche such as Oatly and silken tofu instead of cream cheese.

6
MONTHS
PLUS

DIPS

Crunchy food always tastes better when it is dipped in a delicious sauce. These dips are a brilliant way of supercharging a simple meal.

COCONUT YOGHURT & LIME

A yummy dairy-free dip, perfect with Coconut & Sunflower Seed Chicken Fingers (see page 116) or as a vegan dip for falafels.

MAKES 1 SMALL BOWL – SERVES 2–3 CHILDREN
2–3 tbsp coconut yoghurt
Zest of ½ lime and 2 tsp lime juice

Simply combine all the ingredients together in a small bowl.

STORAGE

Can be stored in a sealed container in the fridge for 3 days, or in the freezer for up to 3 months.

ZESTY LEMON & PESTO

A delicious dip that you will use over and over again. A perfect accompaniment to Lentil Chicken Nuggets (see page 119).

MAKES 1 SMALL BOWL – SERVES 2–3 CHILDREN
2–3 tbsp natural live yoghurt
1 tsp Pumpkin Seed Pesto (see page 121)
    or shop-bought pesto
Zest of ½ lemon and 2 tsp lemon juice

Simply combine all the ingredients together in a small bowl.

STORAGE

Can be stored in a sealed container in the fridge for 3 days, or in the freezer in ice cube trays for up to 3 months.

DAIRY-FREE
Use coconut yoghurt.

LEMON & DILL

Creamy and fresh with tummy-soothing dill, a delicious dip to be paired with Salmon & Cod Potato Fish Cakes (see page 147).

(see page 147)

MAKES 1 SMALL BOWL – SERVES 2-3 CHILDREN
2 tbsp natural live yoghurt
1 tsp fresh lemon juice
1 tsp finely chopped fresh dill
¼ tsp horseradish cream

Simply combine all the ingredients in a small bowl.

To give it a tangier flavour, grate a little lemon zest into the mixture.

STORAGE

Can be stored in a sealed container in the fridge for 3 days, or in the freezer in ice cube trays for up to 3 months.

DAIRY-FREE
Use coconut yoghurt and dairy-free horseradish.

TAHINI & HERB

A calcium-rich dip that works beautifully with Carrot & Apricot Falafels (see page 151).

(see page 151)

MAKES 1 SMALL BOWL – SERVES 2-3 CHILDREN
6 tsp light tahini paste
5 tbsp natural live yoghurt
3 tsp dried mixed herbs

Simply combine all the ingredients in a small bowl.

STORAGE

Can be stored in a sealed container in the fridge for 3 days. Not suitable for freezing.

SESAME-FREE
Swap tahini paste for cashew butter or sunflower seed butter, or leave out.

DAIRY-FREE
Use coconut yoghurt.

CHAPTER TWO

FRUITY WEANING FOODS

Fruit is a healthy way of providing the sweet hit that most kids crave. These blends all have a nutritious twist, with added protein, fibre or fatty acids, making them more filling and thus preventing sugar highs and lows. They can be blended, puréed or turned into smoothies and ice lollies. All suitable from 6 months.

SMOOTHIE BOWLS

STRAWBERRY CHEESECAKE

A luscious bowl of goodness that is a whole meal in one! Decorate it with slices of banana and strawberry to make it look even more appealing.

SERVES 1 ADULT & 1 CHILD
4 strawberries, hulled
1 banana
25g/¼ cup fine porridge oats
¼ avocado, peeled and stoned
¼ tsp vanilla extract
1 tsp cream cheese
Squeeze of fresh lemon juice

Place all the ingredients in a food processor and blitz for 1 minute until smooth.

DAIRY-FREE
Swap cream cheese for cashew butter.

LEMON & BLUEBERRY

Blueberries are incredibly nutritious and full of polyphenols. Combined with bananas and kefir, they make a delicious, thick and creamy smoothie. Top with Lemon & Apricot Granola (see page 81), sliced banana and some extra berries for toddlers.

SERVES 1 ADULT & 1 CHILD
½ banana
50g/¼ cup blueberries
25g/¼ cup fine porridge oats
60ml/¼ cup kefir or Greek-style yoghurt
Zest and juice of ½ lemon

Place all the ingredients in a food processor and blitz for 1 minute until smooth.

GLUTEN-FREE
Use gluten-free oats.

DAIRY-FREE
Swap kefir for coconut yoghurt.

STORAGE

Can be stored in a sealed container in the fridge for 24 hours, or in the freezer for up to 3 months.

PUDDING BOWLS

MANGO, AVOCADO & CHIA

This delicious fruity pudding packs a healthy punch – mangos and avocados are rich in vitamins, while chia seeds contain calcium and omega 3, and turmeric is a natural anti-inflammatory.

SERVES 1 ADULT & 1 CHILD
¼ avocado, peeled and stoned
½ mango, peeled and stoned
1 tsp chia seeds
¼ tsp ground turmeric

Place all the ingredients in a food processor and blitz for 1 minute until smooth.

STORAGE

Can be stored in a sealed container in the fridge for 24 hours, or in the freezer for up to 3 months.

STRAWBERRY, PEACH & ALMOND

Strawberries and peaches taste amazing together, and ground almonds add a little calcium, protein and healthy fat to this yummy little pud.

SERVES 1 ADULT & 1 CHILD
4 strawberries, hulled
1 fresh peach (or nectarine), stoned, or 4 slices tinned peach
4 tsp ground almonds

Place all the ingredients in a food processor and blitz for 1 minute until smooth.

NUT-FREE
Use ground pumpkin or hulled hemp seeds instead of almonds.

BLUEBERRY, VANILLA & CHICKPEA PURÉE

A subtle combination of sweet and savoury – and a great way to get some calcium and fibre into your children!

SERVES 1 ADULT & 1 CHILD
50g/¼ cup blueberries
1 pear, peeled and cored
30g/2 heaped tbsp tinned
   chickpeas, rinsed and drained
½ tsp light tahini paste
¼ tsp vanilla extract

Place all the ingredients in a food processor and blitz for 1 minute until smooth.

SESAME-FREE
Swap tahini paste
for 1 tsp sunflower
butter, cream cheese
or silken tofu, or
simply leave out.

BANANA & MANGO TOFU DELIGHT

Silken tofu is a wonderful source of plant-based calcium and iron. It pairs really well with tropical fruits. This is our favourite combination.

SERVES 1 ADULT & 1 CHILD
½ mango, peeled and stoned
½ banana
125g/¼ cup silken tofu, drained

Place all the ingredients in a food processor and blitz for 1 minute until smooth.

SOYA-FREE
Replace tofu with
natural yoghurt or
coconut yoghurt.

6 MONTHS PLUS

STORAGE

Can be stored in a sealed container in the fridge for 24 hours, or in the freezer for up to 3 months.

SMASHED PLUM & COTTAGE CHEESE

Cottage cheese naturally contains vitamin K, which can help with bruising if your little one has had a bump. The hemp seeds add some healthy omega 3 but you could swap them for sunflower or flax seeds, or leave them out altogether.

SERVES 1 ADULT & 1 CHILD

2 plums, stoned
4 tbsp cottage cheese
1 heaped tsp hulled
    hemp seeds

STORAGE

Can be stored in a sealed container in the fridge for 3 days. Does not freeze well.

Place the plums in a food processor and blitz for a few seconds.

Tip the cottage cheese into a bowl, add the plums and hemp seeds, and fold them together. For newly weaned babies, blitz everything in the food processor for 1 minute until smooth.

DAIRY-FREE
Swap cottage cheese for silken tofu or coconut yoghurt.

COCONUT & PEACH RICE PUDDING

Coconut adds a lovely natural sweetness to this traditional nursery food, eliminating the need for refined sugars. This hob version is much quicker to make, too, and works equally well as a breakfast. You can try different grains, such as quinoa or amaranth, which contain more protein. Top with fresh fruit, a drizzle of maple syrup or some Mango Chia Jam (see page 192).

SERVES 1 ADULT & 1 CHILD

50g/¼ cup short-grain rice or paella rice
480ml/2 cups coconut milk (tinned or fresh)
1 fresh peach (or nectarine), stoned, or 4 tinned peach slices
½ tsp vanilla extract
½ tsp freshly grated nutmeg

Soak the rice and wash thoroughly to remove any impurities.

Place all the ingredients in a small saucepan over a medium heat. Simmer gently for 30–35 minutes, or until the rice is soft, stirring regularly. Add a little more coconut milk towards the end, if needed.

STORAGE

Can be stored in a sealed container in the fridge for 24 hours, or in the freezer for up to 3 months. Can be eaten cold or reheated once.

6
MONTHS
PLUS

RASPBERRY, SWEET POTATO & CARDAMOM BLISS

Cardamom is a lovely Eastern spice that is helpful for digestion and upset tummies. It's a perfect spice to bring sweet and savoury flavours together.

SERVES 1 ADULT & 1 CHILD

12 raspberries
½ medium sweet potato,
    peeled and steamed
60ml/¼ cup coconut milk
1 tsp pumpkin seeds
½ cardamom pod
    (seeds only)

STORAGE

Can be stored in a sealed container in the fridge for 3 days, or in the freezer for up to 3 months.

Place all the ingredients in a food processor and blitz for 1 minute until smooth.

PEAR, CINNAMON & BUTTERNUT SQUASH PURÉE

This is a good recipe for using up leftover butternut squash. Veg dodgers won't even notice it in this naturally sweet and comforting purée.

SERVES 1 ADULT & 1 CHILD

35g butternut squash, peeled and cubed
2 pears, peeled and cored
½ tsp ground cinnamon
1 tsp almond butter

Steam the butternut squash for 15 minutes, or until soft. Leave to cool.

Place the cooled squash in a food processor with all the other ingredients and blitz until smooth.

STORAGE

Can be stored in a sealed container in the fridge for 3 days, or in the freezer for up to 3 months.

6 MONTHS PLUS

NUT-FREE
Swap almond butter for light tahini or sunflower seed butter.

HAPPY TUMMY BLUEBERRY KEFIR

Kefir is a fermented drink similar to yoghurt that has been proven to benefit gut health. I recommend giving it to your kids daily for a few weeks after a course of antibiotics to restore the good bacteria in the gut. Kefir contains lactobacillus, which helps with milk digestion and constipation. I have included prunes and flax seeds in this recipe, too, as they work in harmony to soften stools and keep bowels regular – perfect for kids who get bunged up easily!

SERVES 2 CHILDREN

100g/½ cup fresh or
   frozen blueberries
3 pitted prunes
1 tsp flax seeds
3 tbsp kefir or natural
   Greek-style yoghurt

Place all the ingredients in a food processor and blitz for 1 minute to make a thick purée.

The mixture can also be frozen and made into mini ice-lollies to soothe babies' gums and toddlers will love them too.

STORAGE

Can be stored in a sealed container in the fridge for 3–4 days, or in the freezer for up to 3 months.

DAIRY-FREE
Use coconut, cashew or almond yoghurt instead of kefir.

6 MONTHS PLUS

CHAPTER THREE

BRILLIANT FAMILY BREAKFASTS

Breakfast is the most important meal of the day for children and it's a great chance to pack in the nutrition at a time when they are usually on best form. These are recipes that the whole family can enjoy together.

CARROT CAKE PORRIDGE

This is a yummy recipe that is a hit with all ages, from weaning babies to teenagers. A fantastic way to give kids two of their 'five-a-day', along with nutritious oats, which are full of calcium and beta glucans for immunity.

SERVES 1 ADULT & 1 CHILD

25g/¼ cup fine
    porridge oats
½ small carrot, peeled
    and finely grated
½ small apple, finely
    grated (peeled for babies
    under 12 months)
240ml/1 cup milk
    of choice
1 tsp ground mixed
    sunflower and
    pumpkin seeds
Pinch of ground cinnamon
Pinch of freshly
    grated nutmeg

Place all the ingredients in a small saucepan over a medium heat. Cook for a few minutes, stirring from time to time, until the liquid is absorbed and the porridge is nice and thick.

TIP Blitz enough seeds for several portions in a food processor with a grinding blade and store them in a glass jar in the fridge. You will also find ground mixed seeds in the wholefood section of most supermarkets.

GLUTEN-FREE
Use gluten-free oats.

STORAGE

Can be stored in a sealed container in the fridge for 1–2 days and reheated when needed, adding a little extra milk to loosen. Suitable for freezing, unless using infant milk formula.

6 MONTHS PLUS

CARROT CAKE

SPICED ORANGE QUINOA

BLACKBERRY & PEAR MILLET

SPICED ORANGE QUINOA PORRIDGE

A warming and nutritious breakfast that is suitable from early weaning. The quinoa and almond butter both provide protein, while the cardamom and orange are natural sweeteners. If you don't have quinoa flakes, use porridge oats, buckwheat flakes or amaranth instead – they all work equally well.

SERVES 1 ADULT & 1 CHILD

1 small carrot,
 peeled and grated
Zest and juice of
 1 small orange
30g/¼ cup quinoa flakes
120ml/½ cup milk
 of choice
1 tsp almond butter
Pinch of ground
 cardamom
Small handful of
 cranberries, chopped

Place all the ingredients in a small saucepan over a medium heat. Cook for a few minutes, stirring from time to time, until the liquid is absorbed and the porridge is nice and thick.

NUT-FREE
Swap almond butter
for light tahini paste,
sunflower seed butter,
ground mixed seeds,
or leave out.

STORAGE

Can be stored in a sealed container in the fridge for 1–2 days and reheated when needed, adding a little extra milk to loosen. Suitable for freezing, unless using infant milk formula.

6
MONTHS
PLUS

BLACKBERRY & PEAR MILLET PORRIDGE

Blackberry, pear and vanilla make such a delicious combination. Millet is a nutrient-dense grain that is naturally rich in prebiotics. It boosts the gut microbiome and is particularly helpful for regulating loose bowels, and so is a good choice for little ones with explosive nappies! Millet flakes are available in most health food shops or online, but you could use fine porridge oats, quinoa flakes or buckwheat flakes.

SERVES 1 ADULT & 1 CHILD

1 pear, peeled,
   cored and grated
10–12 fresh or frozen
   blackberries
30g/¼ cup millet flakes
120ml/½ cup milk
   of choice
½ tsp vanilla extract
1 tsp cashew butter

Place all the ingredients in a small saucepan over a medium heat. Cook for a few minutes, stirring from time to time, until the liquid is absorbed and the porridge is nice and thick.

NUT-FREE
Swap cashew butter
for light tahini paste,
sunflower seed butter,
ground mixed seeds,
or leave out.

STORAGE

Can be stored in a sealed container in the fridge for 1–2 days and reheated when needed, adding a little extra milk to loosen. Suitable for freezing, unless using infant milk formula.

6
MONTHS
PLUS

APPLE & CINNAMON OVERNIGHT OATS

This is a speedy breakfast that you can prepare the night before. The oats soak up the juice from the apple and the yoghurt overnight and the raisins become softer and more digestible. It's based on a traditional Swiss recuperation recipe that you can give your little one after illness to help restore the beneficial probiotic bacteria that are so important for immunity and overall health.

SERVES 1 ADULT & 1 CHILD

30g/¼ cup porridge oats
120ml/½ cup milk
   of choice
75ml/⅓ cup kefir or
   natural Greek-style
   yoghurt
1 apple, cored and
   finely grated (peeled
   for children under
   12 months)
2 tsp raisins or sultanas
1 tsp sunflower seeds
¼ tsp ground cinnamon

Simply mix all the ingredients together in a bowl before bedtime and pop in the fridge overnight.

In the morning, give the mixture a quick stir and add some extra yoghurt to loosen, if needed.

On chilly mornings, place in a small saucepan over a gentle heat to warm through.

STORAGE

Can be stored in a sealed container in the fridge for 1–2 days. Suitable for freezing, unless using infant milk formula.

DAIRY-FREE
Swap kefir for coconut, cashew or almond yoghurt.

GLUTEN-FREE
Use gluten-free oats.

6 MONTHS PLUS

NUT-FREE BREAKFAST SQUARES

A grabbable breakfast for those mornings when you're rushing out the door. It's packed full of vitamins and minerals that will help fight off any lurking bugs. Perfect for a mid-morning snack or for your older children's lunch boxes, too.

MAKES 25 MINI SQUARES

90g pitted dates
100g/¾ cup sunflower seeds
100g/¾ cup pumpkin seeds
300g/3–4 bananas
2 tsp light tahini paste
Zest and juice of 1 orange
200g/2 cups fine porridge oats
1 medium carrot, peeled and finely grated
5mm fresh root ginger, peeled and grated, or ½ tsp ground ginger
2 tsp ground cinnamon
1 tsp vanilla extract or seeds from 1 vanilla pod

Preheat the oven to 180°C/160°C fan/gas mark 4 and line a 20cm square baking tin with parchment paper.

Soak the dates in boiling water for 5 minutes, then drain and finely chop.

Pulse the sunflower and pumpkin seeds in a food processor until coarsely ground.

In a large mixing bowl, mash the bananas and tahini to a soft purée, then stir in the orange zest and juice.

Add the oats, chopped seeds, dates, grated carrot, ginger, cinnamon and vanilla to the bowl and mix well until combined – it will become a thick dough.

Spread the mixture into the prepared baking tin, pressing down with the back of a spoon until nicely compacted, and bake in the oven for 20–22 minutes.

Remove from the oven and leave to cool before cutting into 25 squares.

STORAGE

Can be stored in an airtight container for 4 days, or in the freezer for up to 2 months.

12 MONTHS PLUS

GLUTEN-FREE
Use gluten-free oats.

SESAME-FREE
Swap tahini paste for sunflower butter or leave out.

LEMON & APRICOT GRANOLA

The whole family will love this zingy granola. Serve with milk or yoghurt
for breakfast, or as a topping for smoothie bowls (see page 61). Try to
source unsulphured apricots, if possible, as they are additive-free.

MAKES 10-12 SERVINGS

2 tbsp maple syrup
4 tbsp coconut oil
1 tbsp coconut sugar or
    light muscovado sugar
Zest of 1 lemon
300g/3 cups porridge oats
30g/¼ cup pumpkin
    seeds
30g/¼ cup sunflower
    seeds
60g dried apricots
    (ideally unsulphured),
    roughly chopped

STORAGE

Can be stored in an
airtight container
for up to 6 weeks.

12
MONTHS
PLUS

Preheat the oven to 200°C/180°C fan/gas mark 5.

Place the maple syrup and coconut oil in a small
saucepan and melt together over a gentle heat.

Meanwhile, place the sugar in a large bowl, add the
lemon zest and rub together between your fingers
so the flavours infuse.

Tip the oats and seeds into the bowl with the lemon
sugar, then stir in the maple syrup mixture, until
everything has an even coating.

Spread the granola in a thin layer across a baking tray
and bake for 20–25 minutes, shaking the tray every
5 minutes or so, until the oats have a light, even colour.

Remove from the oven and sprinkle over the apricots.
Leave to cool before storing in an airtight container.

GLUTEN-FREE
Use gluten-free oats.

RASPBERRY BANANA PANCAKES

A gorgeous soft pancake suitable for babies who can feed themselves, even if they don't have many teeth! The ground almonds and eggs provide lots of healthy calcium, vitamin D, vitamin B12 and iron.

MAKES 6–8 MINI PANCAKES

1 banana, mashed
2 free-range eggs
50g/½ cup ground
   almonds
10–12 fresh or frozen
   raspberries, plus
   extra to serve
Small knob of
   unsalted butter

STORAGE

Can be stored in the fridge for 2 days, or in the freezer for up to 3 months.

6 MONTHS PLUS

Place the mashed banana, eggs, almonds and raspberries in a medium bowl and mix well to make a batter.

Place a non-stick frying pan over a medium heat and add the butter.

Dollop heaped teaspoonfuls of batter into the pan, 2–3 at a time. Fry for 1–2 minutes on each side, or until golden brown.

Repeat until you have 6–8 mini pancakes.

Serve with more berries and a drizzle of maple syrup.

NUT-FREE
Swap the ground almonds for 1 tbsp tahini paste, cream cheese or silken tofu.

DAIRY-FREE
Use dairy-free spread or olive oil instead of butter.

EGG-FREE
Swap the egg for 1 heaped tsp chickpea (gram) flour and 3 tsp water.

COTTAGE CHEESE & DILL BLINIS

These mini blinis are a lovely savoury breakfast and a cinch to make.
For alternative toppings, try the Zingy Hummus Trio (see page 47),
Trout & Dill Pâté (see page 55), Mexican Black Bean Pâté (see page 50)
or Sage & Cranberry Chicken Liver Pâté (see page 103).

MAKES 18 MINI BLINIS

160g cottage cheese
50g/½ cup porridge oats
2 free-range eggs
¾ tsp baking powder
Freshly ground black
   pepper (optional)
Pinch of fine sea
   (not for children
   under 12 months)
1 spring onion,
   finely chopped
Sprig of dill, chopped,
   plus extra to garnish,
   or a pinch of dried
2 slices smoked salmon
   (or flaked poached
   salmon for children
   under 12 months)

Place 120g of the cottage cheese, the porridge oats, eggs and baking powder in a food processor and whizz until you have a smooth batter. Season, if using, then stir in the spring onion and dill. Leave the batter to stand for a few minutes.

Place a non-stick frying pan over a medium heat and place heaped teaspoonfuls of the batter in the pan – aim for 3 blinis at a time. Once they start to bubble, flip them over. When the blinis are golden on both sides, transfer them to a plate. Repeat until you have 18 mini blinis.

To serve, top each blini with ½ teaspoon cottage cheese, a small piece of salmon and a sprinkle of dill.

STORAGE

Can be stored in the fridge for 2 days, or in the freezer for up to 3 months. Place a small square of baking paper between each one, so they are easy to defrost individually.

6 MONTHS PLUS

DAIRY-FREE
Replace cottage cheese with silken tofu or cashew butter.

EGG-FREE
Swap eggs for 2 tbsp ground flax seeds combined with 6 tbsp water.

GLUTEN-FREE
Use gluten-free oats and baking powder.

CHEESY COURGETTE

BEETROOT BERRY

CHICKPEA WAFFLES 2 WAYS

If your child is drawn to crunchy, beige food, then these waffles are just the trick. Packed with goodness, they make a meal-in-one any time of the day, or are a great snack to grab from the freezer and toast from frozen.

CHEESY COURGETTE

MAKES 7 WAFFLES

160g/1 cup spelt or wholemeal flour
160g/1 cup chickpea (gram) flour
300ml/1¼ cups milk of choice
½ courgette, finely grated
100g Cheddar, grated
4–6 chives, finely chopped
1 tsp unsalted butter, melted, or olive oil

Place all the ingredients in a large bowl and mix together – no need to make the batter too smooth.

Turn your waffle maker to a medium-high setting and pour a ladleful of the mixture into the lower plate. Be careful not to overfill it or the mixture will come pouring out of the sides. Close the lid and let the waffle cook for 5 minutes. Repeat until you have used up all the batter.

STORAGE

Can be stored in an airtight container for 7 days, or in the freezer for up to 3 months.

DAIRY-FREE
Use silken tofu or cashew butter plus 1 heaped tsp nutritional yeast, or a hard vegan cheese instead of Cheddar.

BEETROOT BERRY

MAKES 7 WAFFLES

160g/1 cup spelt or wholemeal flour
160g/1 cup chickpea (gram) flour
300ml/1¼ cups milk of choice
1 small beetroot, cooked without vinegar
100g fresh or frozen raspberries
50g/¼ cup cream cheese
60ml/¼ cup maple syrup

Place all the ingredients in a large bowl and blitz using a hand blender – no need to make the batter too smooth.

Turn your waffle maker to the medium-high setting and pour a ladleful of the mixture into the lower plate. Be careful not to overfill it or the mixture will come pouring out of the sides. Close the lid and let the waffle cook for 5 minutes. Repeat until you have used up all the batter.

TIP Chickpea flour, also known as gram or besan flour, can be found on the Asian food shelves of most supermarkets. You can make your own by blitzing dried chickpeas in a food processor with a grinding blade for about 1 minute. Note: Never eat raw chickpea flour.

GLUTEN-FREE
Use gluten-free flour.

DAIRY-FREE
Use silken tofu or cashew butter instead of cream cheese.

BLUEBERRY & BANANA BAKED OATS

Sweet, soft and chewy, these baked oats are suitable for the whole family, even for weaning babies from 6 months (once they've got the hang of finger food). They make a delicious breakfast, snack or pudding, and any leftovers can be frozen. Oats are full of calcium and immune-supporting beta glucans. The egg and the milk provide protein, as well as choline, which is an important brain food.

MAKES 6-8 SERVINGS

Unsalted butter or
coconut oil, for greasing
3 bananas
240ml/1 cup milk
of choice
2 free-range eggs
200g/2 cups fine
porridge oats
1 tsp baking powder
1 heaped tsp mixed spice
1 tbsp honey (not for
children under 12
months) or maple syrup
100g/½ cup fresh or
frozen blueberries

Preheat the oven to 180°C/160°C fan /gas mark 4 and grease a medium baking dish.

Place 2 bananas in a large bowl and mash with a fork. Slice the remaining banana into 3 lengthways and set aside.

Add the milk and eggs to the bowl with the mashed banana and mix well. Stir in the oats, baking powder, mixed spice and honey or maple syrup, followed by the blueberries.

Pour the mixture into the prepared baking dish and arrange the banana slices on top. Bake for 40–45 minutes, or until golden brown.

Serve warm with natural Greek-style yoghurt, or leave to cool.

STORAGE

Can be stored in an airtight container for 4 days, or in the freezer for up to 3 months.

6 MONTHS PLUS

GLUTEN-FREE
Use gluten-free oats
and baking powder.

EGG-FREE
Swap eggs for 2 tbsp
ground flax seeds
combined with
4 tbsp water.

SWEET POTATO, BANANA & CRANBERRY MUFFINS

A filling and nutritious breakfast or teatime treat. It's the perfect snack to take with you when you're out and about.

MAKES 12 MUFFINS

3 free-range eggs
70g/⅓ cup coconut
    sugar or light
    muscovado sugar
1 medium sweet potato,
    peeled and finely grated
1 banana, mashed
160g/1 cup spelt or
    wholemeal flour
100g/1 cup ground
    almonds
1 heaped tsp ground
    cinnamon
2 tsp baking powder
½ tsp bicarbonate of soda
¼ tsp fine sea salt
    (not for children
    under 12 months)
25g/¼ cup dried
    cranberries
25g/¼ cup pumpkin seeds
    (ground for babies and
    fussy kids)

Preheat the oven to 180°C/160°C fan/gas mark 4 and line a muffin tin with 12 paper cases.

Whisk the eggs and sugar together in a large bowl for 3 minutes using an electric whisk, or until the mixture is nice and creamy.

Gently stir in the grated sweet potato and mashed banana.

Fold in the flour, ground almonds, cinnamon, baking powder, bicarbonate of soda and salt, if using. Take care not to over-stir to keep the mixture light.

Finally, fold in the cranberries and pumpkin seeds.

Divide the muffin mixture between the paper cases and bake in the oven for 25 minutes, or until they have risen and the tops are golden brown.

STORAGE

Can be stored in an airtight container for 7 days, or in the freezer for up to 3 months.

EGG-FREE
Swap eggs for 3 tbsp ground flax seeds combined with 7½ tbsp water.

GLUTEN-FREE
Use rice flour or gluten-free plain flour and baking powder.

NUT-FREE
Replace the almonds with 160g sunflower seeds ground to a flour in a food processor.

CHEESE & APPLE EGGY BREAD

A tasty savoury breakfast that is quick to make and soft enough
for small babies.

SERVES 1 CHILD

1 free-range egg
½ apple, grated
(peeled for babies
under 12 months)
20g Gruyère, grated
1 slice wholemeal or
sourdough bread
Knob of unsalted butter
or coconut oil (with a
neutral taste), for frying

Crack the egg into a wide, flat bowl and beat in the grated
apple and cheese.

Dip the bread into the egg mixture, making sure it gets
an even coating.

Melt the butter or coconut oil in a heavy-based frying
pan over a medium heat. Place the bread in the pan and
fry for 3–4 minutes on each side, or until golden brown.

Cut into soldiers to serve.

STORAGE

Once cooked, it will keep
in the fridge for 24 hours.
Does not freeze well.

6 MONTHS PLUS

EGG-FREE
Swap egg for
a banana blended
with 50ml milk.

DAIRY-FREE
Use a hard
vegan cheese.

GLUTEN-FREE
Use gluten-free
wholemeal or
sourdough bread.

SCRAMBLED EGGS WITH RED PEPPER & CHIVES

A healthier twist on traditional scrambled eggs, this dish goes well with Kefir Flatbreads (see page 132) or Yellow Split Pea Flatbread (see page 114).

SERVES 1–2 CHILDREN

Knob of unsalted butter
¼ red pepper, deseeded and finely chopped
½ tsp mixed dried Mediterranean herbs
2 free-range eggs, lightly beaten
1–2 chives, finely chopped
Freshly ground black pepper (optional)
Pinch of fine sea salt (not for children under 12 months)

Melt the butter in a small non-stick saucepan over a medium heat.

Add the red pepper and herbs and fry for 3 minutes.

Add the beaten eggs and chopped chives and cook, stirring with a silicone spatula, until the eggs have scrambled. Add seasoning, if using, and serve.

STORAGE

Always cook to serve. Does not freeze well.

6 MONTHS PLUS

EGG-FREE
Swap eggs for silken tofu and ½ tsp ground turmeric.

DAIRY-FREE
Use 1 tsp olive oil instead of butter.

EGGY SALMON & DILL MUFFINS

Oily fish, like salmon, are a great source of omega 3, which is one of the most important nutrients for a baby's brain. The eggs and cheese in these muffins also provide essential protein.

MAKES 4 LARGE OR 8 MINI MUFFINS

2 free-range eggs
½ salmon fillet, skin
removed, cut into
2–4cm chunks
1 tbsp cream cheese
Sprig of dill, chopped,
or 1 tsp dried
Zest of ½ lemon

STORAGE

Always cook to serve.
These do not freeze well.

Preheat the oven to 180°C/160°C fan/gas mark 4 and place a silicon muffin tray on a baking tray to stabilise it. (If you are using a metal muffin tin, place it in the oven to heat up.)

Crack the eggs into a bowl and lightly whisk with a fork.

Gently stir in the salmon, cream cheese, dill and lemon zest.

Remove the tray from the oven and pour the mixture into the muffin holes until they are two-thirds full. Bake in the oven for 10–12 minutes, depending on their size, or until set.

EGG-FREE
Use Orgran Vegan
Easy Egg.

DAIRY-FREE
Replace cream cheese
with an oat crème fraîche,
such as Oatly, or vegan
cream cheese.

APPLEY BAKED BEANS

This will become one of your family staples. Once you have tried these, you'll never buy a tin of baked beans again.

SERVES 3-4 CHILDREN

1 tsp olive oil
1 celery stick, diced
1 small carrot, peeled
    and diced
240ml/1 cup passata
240ml/1 cup vegetable
    or chicken stock
    (homemade or very
    low salt)
2 x 400g tins haricot
    or cannellini beans,
    rinsed and drained
1 small apple, cored and
    grated (peeled for under
    12 months)
1 tsp smoked paprika
1 tsp fresh or dried thyme
1 tsp apple cider vinegar or
    apple balsamic vinegar
Knob of unsalted butter
Freshly ground black
    pepper (optional)
Pinch of fine sea salt
    (not for children
    under 12 months)

Place the olive oil in a saucepan over a medium heat. Add the celery and carrot and fry for 1 minute.

Stir in all the remaining the ingredients, except the butter and seasoning. Reduce the heat and simmer for 40 minutes, stirring every now and then.

When the sauce has reduced and the carrots are soft, stir in the butter and season, if using.

Serve on toast, as a filling for a baked potato, or with scrambled eggs and sausages.

CELERY-FREE
Replace with fennel
or leave out.

DAIRY-FREE
Use olive oil
instead of butter.

STORAGE

Can be stored in a sealed container in the fridge for 3 days, or in the freezer for up to 3 months.

PARSNIP & BANANA BREAD

This is the only way I can get parsnip into my youngest son – and he loves this bread! Super-light, fluffy and delicately spiced, it is a perfect teatime snack, as well as at breakfast.

MAKES 1 LOAF

240g/1½ cups spelt
   or wholemeal flour
75g/¾ cup fine
   porridge oats
25g coconut sugar or
   light muscovado sugar
½ tsp ground cinnamon
½ tsp freshly grated
   nutmeg
½ tsp ground allspice
1 tsp baking powder
Pinch of fine sea salt
   (not for children
   under 12 months)
120g/1 medium parsnip,
   peeled and coarsely
   grated
2 large bananas, mashed
2 free-range eggs,
   lightly beaten
60ml/¼ cup milk
   of choice
60ml/¼ cup light olive oil
2 tbsp raisins or sultanas

Preheat the oven to 180°C/160°C fan /gas mark 4 and line a 500g loaf tin with parchment paper, using a few dabs of butter or coconut oil to help it stick.

Sift the flour into a large bowl and stir in the oats, sugar, spices, baking powder and salt, if using.

In a separate bowl, combine the parsnip, bananas, eggs, milk and olive oil. Stir in the raisins or sultanas. Add this to the dry ingredients and stir until just combined.

Pour the mixture into the prepared tin and bake for 45–50 minutes, or until a skewer inserted into the middle of the loaf comes out clean.

Remove from the oven and leave to cool in the tin, before transferring to a wire rack.

STORAGE

Can be stored in an airtight container for 3 days, or in the freezer for up to 3 months.

EGG-FREE
Swap eggs for 2 tbsp ground flax seeds combined with 6 tbsp water.

GLUTEN-FREE
Use rice flour or gluten-free plain flour and baking powder.

CHAPTER FOUR

FAMILY LUNCHES & SUPPERS

With recipes that can easily be smooshed up to turn into baby purée as well as dishes for more confident feeders or for babies who are determined to feed themselves, this section is split into two. Think messy pasta and rice dishes that can be served with a spoon or grabbed by a little fist, as well as nuggets, burgers and falafels.

6 MONTHS PLUS

LEMONY CHICKEN & ORZO SOUP

A zingy soup that contains lots of lovely chicken stock, as well as vitamin C-rich lemon juice and parsley. If you can't find orzo (a rice-shaped pasta), you could use pasta letters or stars, rice or pearled spelt. Swap chicken for butterbeans for a plant-based version.

SERVES 2 ADULTS & 3 BABY PORTIONS

2 tbsp olive oil
250g/2–3 boneless, skinless chicken thighs, cut into 4cm strips
2 shallots or 1 small onion, diced
2 garlic cloves, crushed
2 carrots, peeled and diced
1 celery stick, diced
Sprig of rosemary, leaves finely chopped, or 1 tsp dried
Sprig of thyme, leaves chopped, or 1 tsp dried
1 bay leaf
125g/½ cup orzo pasta
500ml/2 cups chicken or vegetable stock (homemade or very low salt)
Juice of ½ lemon
1 heaped tbsp finely chopped fresh parsley
Freshly ground black pepper (optional)
Pinch of fine sea salt (not for children under 12 months)

Place the olive oil in a large saucepan over a high heat. Add the chicken and brown all over. Remove with a slotted spoon and set aside.

Add the shallots or onion to the pan, reduce the heat and fry for 3–5 minutes, or until soft, adding a little more olive oil if necessary. Add the garlic and cook for a further minute.

Stir in the carrots, celery and herbs, and cook for another minute.

Stir in the orzo, browned chicken and stock, and continue to cook for 11–12 minutes, or until the orzo is soft and the chicken is cooked through.

Remove from the heat and stir in the lemon juice, parsley and seasoning, if using, to serve.

If you want to purée some for a young baby, spoon a portion into a jug and blitz with a hand blender for 2 minutes.

CELERY-FREE
Replace with fennel or leave out.

GLUTEN-FREE
Use gluten-free mini pasta shapes, white rice or red lentil or legume rice.

TUSCAN SPELT & BORLOTTI BEAN SOUP

Spelt is an ancient Italian grain that is easier to digest than modern wheat, so it's a good first food for delicate tummies. Its nutty flavour combines beautifully with the beans to make a thick and wholesome chunky soup that can be blended into a purée. If you can't find quick-cook spelt, use pearled spelt, rice, orzo or legume rice, and adjust the cooking time accordingly.

SERVES 2 ADULTS & 3 BABY PORTIONS

2 tbsp olive oil
1 onion, diced
1 garlic clove, crushed
1 carrot, peeled and diced
1 celery stick, diced
90g/½ cup quick-cook
    pearled spelt
1 × 400g tin borlotti beans,
    rinsed and drained
1 litre chicken or vegetable
    stock (homemade or
    very low salt)
1 heaped tbsp
    tomato purée
Sprig of rosemary,
    leaves finely chopped,
    or 1 tsp dried
Freshly ground black
    pepper (optional)
Pinch of fine sea salt
    (not for children
    under 12 months)
Small handful of kale
    leaves, roughly chopped
10–15g Parmesan, grated

Place the oil in a large saucepan over a low to medium heat, add the onion and fry for 3–5 minutes, or until soft. Add the garlic and cook for a further minute.

Stir in the remaining ingredients, except the kale and Parmesan, and bring to the boil.

Reduce the heat and simmer for 11 minutes, or until the spelt is soft. Stir the kale leaves into the soup 3 minutes before the end of the cooking time.

If you want to purée some for a young baby, spoon a portion into a jug and blitz with a hand blender for 2 minutes.

Sprinkle with Parmesan to serve.

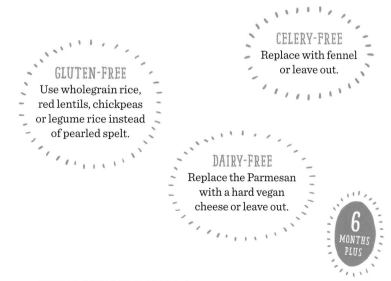

STORAGE

Can be stored in a sealed container in the fridge for 3–4 days, or in the freezer for up to 3 months. Can be reheated once.

CELERY-FREE
Replace with fennel
or leave out.

GLUTEN-FREE
Use wholegrain rice,
red lentils, chickpeas
or legume rice instead
of pearled spelt.

DAIRY-FREE
Replace the Parmesan
with a hard vegan
cheese or leave out.

6
MONTHS
PLUS

SAGE & CRANBERRY CHICKEN LIVER PÂTÉ

Bursting with protein, iron and choline, chicken livers are a wonderfully nutritious food, while both sage and cranberry are natural antimicrobials. Spread the pâté on toast or crackers, or stir into mince dishes, such as Supercharged Beef & Lentil Ragu (see page 126). Note: You should limit liver to about 3 teaspoons (15g) a week for babies under 12 months as it is high in vitamin A. Liver is unsuitable during pregnancy.

SERVES 6-8

1 shallot or ½ small onion, finely chopped
2 tbsp clarified unsalted butter or ghee, melted, plus 1 heaped tsp
400g chicken livers
1 apple, peeled, cored and grated
2–3 sage leaves or 1 tsp dried
1 heaped tsp dried cranberries
Freshly ground black pepper (optional)
Pinch of fine sea salt (not for children under 12 months)

STORAGE

Can be stored in a sealed container in the fridge for up to 7 days, or in the freezer for up to 3 months.

Place the onion in a small saucepan with the heaped teaspoon of the butter or ghee and fry over a medium heat for 3–5 minutes, or until soft and translucent.

Meanwhile, trim the chicken livers of any stringy sinews, then rinse and gently pat dry with kitchen paper. Dice into very small pieces and add to the onion.

Stir in the apple and sage and cook for 3–4 minutes, or until the apple is soft and the livers are no longer pink.

Transfer the mixture to a food processor or blender, add the cranberries and pulse for around 1 minute, or until you have a smooth consistency. Add seasoning, if using.

Transfer the pâté to a glass jar and top with the melted butter or ghee to seal it. A whole sage leaf suspended in the ghee adds a decorative touch!

TIP To make your own ghee, melt 2 tablespoons butter, skimming the white froth off the top with a slotted spoon as it bubbles. Use any leftover ghee in curries or dhal.

DAIRY-FREE
Swap butter for goose or duck fat or coconut oil.

MINI PASTA SHAPES WITH A VEGGIE SAUCE

A tomato-flavoured sauce is a clever way to hide veggies for fussy eaters. Serve it chunky for older children or puréed for little ones.

SERVES 3–4 CHILDREN

1 tbsp olive oil
½ onion, diced
1 garlic clove, crushed
1 × 400 tin chopped
    tomatoes
600ml/2½ cups chicken
    or vegetable stock
    (homemade or
    very low salt)
200g/1 cup red lentils
1 carrot, peeled and diced
1 celery stick, diced
1 small sweet potato,
    peeled and diced
Sprig of oregano,
    leaves finely chopped,
    or 1 tsp dried
Freshly ground black
    pepper (optional)
Pinch of fine sea salt
    (not for children
    under 12 months)
Mini pasta shapes (15g per
    baby or 25g per toddler)
15–20g Cheddar or
    Parmesan, grated

Place the oil in a large saucepan over a low to medium heat, add the onion and fry for 3–5 minutes, or until soft. Add the garlic and cook for a further minute.

Stir in the tomatoes, stock, lentils, carrot, celery, sweet potato, oregano and seasoning, if using. Leave to simmer for about 20 minutes, or until the lentils and veg are tender.

Meanwhile, cook the pasta according to the packet instructions.

Stir the sauce into the pasta. If you want to purée some for a young baby, spoon a portion into a jug and blitz with a hand blender for 2 minutes.

For older children, sprinkle with cheese to serve.

CELERY-FREE
Replace with fennel
or leave out.

STORAGE

Can be stored in a sealed container in the fridge for 3–4 days, or in the freezer for up to 3 months. Can be reheated once.

GREEN LENTIL & SUN-DRIED TOMATO SHEPHERD'S PIE

6 MONTHS PLUS

A perfect family meal for Meat-Free Mondays. For those of you who prefer it meaty, swap the cannellini beans for 400g lamb mince.

SERVES 4 ADULTS & 2 TODDLERS

2 tbsp olive oil
1 onion, diced
1 garlic clove, crushed
500ml/2 cups vegetable
    stock (homemade
    or very low salt)
200g/1 cup green lentils
2 medium carrots,
    peeled and diced
1 celery stick, diced
3 sprigs of thyme, leaves
    chopped, or 1 tsp dried
2 bay leaves
1 × 400g tin cannellini
    beans, rinsed and drained
2 heaped tbsp tomato purée
10 sun-dried tomatoes,
    finely chopped
5 medium white potatoes,
    peeled and cut into chunks
1 small leek, finely chopped
15g unsalted butter
2 tbsp milk of choice
Freshly ground black
    pepper (optional)
Pinch of fine sea salt
    (not for children
    under 12 months)

Preheat the oven to 200°C/180°C fan/gas mark 5.

Place the oil in a saucepan over a medium heat. Add the onion and fry for 3–5 minutes, or until soft. Add the garlic and cook for a further minute.

Stir in the stock, lentils, carrots, celery and herbs. Leave to simmer for about 10 minutes, then add the cannellini beans, tomato purée and sun-dried tomatoes. Cook for about 18 minutes, or until the lentils are soft. Add a little more stock or water, if the mixture is too thick.

Meanwhile, place the potatoes in a large saucepan of water, bring to the boil and cook for 10–15 minutes, or until soft. Drain well, return to the pan and mash.

Place the leek and butter in a small frying pan over a medium heat and fry gently until soft. Stir into the mashed potato, adding a little milk to thin, if needed. Season to taste, if using.

Tip the cannellini bean mixture into a medium pie dish and spread the mash over the top. Bake in the oven for about 20 minutes, or until the potato is golden and starting to crisp.

STORAGE

Can be stored in a sealed container in the fridge for 3–4 days, or in the freezer for up to 3 months.

CELERY-FREE
Replace with fennel
or leave out.

DAIRY-FREE
Use dairy-free spread
instead of butter.

FISH PIE WITH CHEESY POTATO & BROCCOLI MASH

This is true comfort food – a filling dish that includes lots of green veg and a healthy balance of protein, carbs and fats. The fish provides plenty of iodine and omega 3, which are important for brain development and a healthy metabolism.

SERVES 3-4 CHILDREN

2–3 medium white potatoes, peeled and cut into chunks
4–5 broccoli florets
2 tbsp unsalted butter
30g Cheddar, grated
4 spring onions, finely chopped
1 tsp plain wholemeal flour
200ml/¾ cup milk of choice
1 haddock, cod or coley fillet, cut into 2cm cubes
1 salmon fillet, cut into 1cm cubes
Zest of 1 lemon
Large sprig of dill, chopped
Large sprig of parsley, leaves finely chopped
Handful of baby spinach, shredded
Freshly ground black pepper (optional)
Pinch of fine sea salt (not for children under 12 months)

Preheat the oven to 180°C/160°C fan/gas mark 4.

Place the potatoes in a large saucepan, cover with water and bring to the boil. Cook for 10–15 minutes, or until soft.

Meanwhile, steam the broccoli florets for 5–6 minutes, until soft but still vibrant green.

Drain the potatoes and mash with half the butter, the cheese and the broccoli. Set aside.

Melt the remaining butter in another saucepan over a low heat. Add the spring onions and fry gently for 3–5 minutes.

Stir in the flour, then slowly add the milk, stirring constantly to prevent lumps forming. Add the fish and poach for 5 minutes, or until cooked through.

Add the lemon zest, herbs, spinach and seasoning, if using, then pour the fish mixture into a medium ovenproof dish. Spread the mash over the top and bake for 20 minutes, or until the potato is golden brown and starting to crisp.

STORAGE

Can be stored in a sealed container in the fridge for 3–4 days, or in the freezer for up to 3 months.

GLUTEN-FREE
Use gluten-free flour.

DAIRY-FREE
Use dairy-free spread instead of butter, and add 1 heaped tsp nutritional yeast to the mash instead of the cheese.

LAMB, APRICOT & CINNAMON TAGINE

This dish won our toddler taste-off. The spices are perfect for developing young taste buds. Serve it on a bed of Parsley Couscous (see page 110) or with Yellow Split Pea Flatbread (see page 114).

SERVES 6-7 CHILDREN

300g lamb neck fillet, cut into 1–2cm pieces
1 tsp ground cinnamon
½ tsp ground coriander
¼ tsp ground turmeric
¼ tsp ground cumin
5 dried apricots (ideally unsulphured)
3 pitted prunes
3 tbsp olive or coconut oil
1 medium red onion, finely chopped
1 celery stick, diced
½ garlic clove, crushed
1 × 400g tin chickpeas, rinsed and drained
300g/1 small butternut squash, peeled and cut into 1cm cubes
1 large carrot, peeled and diced
250ml/1 cup stock (homemade or very low salt)
Knob of fresh root ginger, peeled and grated
1 tbsp tomato purée
Zest and juice of 1 orange
Freshly ground black pepper (optional)
Pinch of fine sea salt (not for children under 12 months)
1 tbsp finely chopped mint leaves
50g pistachios, chopped, or blitzed for babies

Place the lamb in a large bowl and toss in all the spices. Cover and leave to marinate overnight, or for as long as possible.

Preheat the oven to 160°C/140°C fan/gas mark 2.

Place the apricots and prunes in a small bowl and pour boiling water over the top. Leave to soak for 5 minutes, then drain and finely chop.

Place a flameproof casserole dish over a medium to high heat and add 1 tablespoon of the oil. Add the diced lamb and seal on all sides. Transfer to a plate.

Add the onion, celery and remaining oil to the casserole dish and fry for a few minutes until soft. Add the garlic and fry for a further minute.

Stir in the chickpeas, squash, carrot, apricots, prunes, stock, ginger and tomato purée. Bring to the boil, then return the lamb to the pan and add the orange zest and juice. Cover with a lid and transfer to the oven for 1½ hours, or until the lamb is tender. If you want a thicker sauce, remove the lid for the last 15 minutes of the cooking time. Season to taste, if using, and sprinkle the mint and pistachios on top just before serving.

If you want to purée some for a young baby, spoon a portion into a jug and blitz with a hand blender for 2 minutes.

6 MONTHS PLUS

CELERY-FREE
Replace with fennel or leave out.

STORAGE
Can be stored in a sealed container in the fridge for 3–4 days, or in the freezer for up to 3 months.

PARSLEY COUSCOUS

A simple recipe that makes a versatile accompaniment to lots of dishes.
Parsley is packed with iron and vitamin C, which are both important
for nourishing the immune system.

SERVES 2 ADULTS & 1 CHILD

150g/1 cup couscous
480ml/2 cups
    boiling water
Small handful of finely
    chopped parsley
Splash of olive oil

Place the couscous in a serving bowl. Pour the boiling water over the top and leave to swell and soften for 10 minutes.

Stir in the parsley and olive oil just before serving. Can be served warm or at room temperature.

STORAGE

Can be stored in a sealed container in the fridge for 2–3 days. Not suitable for freezing.

GLUTEN-FREE
Use gluten-free couscous or quinoa.

6
MONTHS
PLUS

TURKEY & CRANBERRY SLEEPY CASSEROLE

Turkey doesn't have to be just for Christmas! It contains tryptophan, an amino acid that helps to regulate sleep – a good reason to eat it all year round. Serve this yummy casserole with wholegrain brown rice or fluffy quinoa, or blend it into a purée with a touch more stock for littlies.

SERVES 5–6 CHILDREN

1 tbsp olive or coconut oil
1 small red onion, diced
1 garlic clove, crushed
250g turkey fillet,
    cut into 1cm cubes
1 medium sweet potato,
    peeled and cut into
    1cm cubes
1 large carrot,
    peeled and diced
50g/½ cup dried
    cranberries
150ml/⅔ cup chicken
    stock (homemade
    or very low salt)
Juice of 1 tangerine
1 tsp fresh tarragon
    leaves, finely chopped,
    or 1 tsp dried
Freshly ground black
    pepper (optional)
Pinch of fine sea salt
    (not for children
    under 12 months)
1 tsp finely chopped
    fresh parsley

Place the oil in a saucepan over a low to medium heat. Add the onion and fry for 3–5 minutes, or until soft. Add the garlic and cook for a further minute.

Turn up the heat and add the turkey to the pan. Stir-fry for 8–10 minutes to seal it on all sides – the meat should turn from pink to white.

Stir in the sweet potato, carrot, cranberries, stock, tangerine juice and tarragon, cover the pan and bring to the boil. Reduce the heat and leave to simmer for 20–25 minutes.

Season to taste, if using, then leave to cool slightly before sprinkling with parsley to serve.

If you want to purée some for a young baby, spoon a portion into a jug and blitz with a hand blender for 2 minutes.

STORAGE

Can be stored in a sealed container in the fridge for 3–4 days, or in the freezer for up to 3 months.

COCONUT & TOMATO LENTIL CURRY

This mild curry is the perfect dish to introduce babies and toddlers to lentils and spices. Lentils contain significant amounts of insoluble fibre, which promotes good digestion. They are also a great source of vitamin B and iron. Of all the lentil dishes tried on our toddler tasting team, this was the one they liked best. Purée it for babies and serve it with brown rice and Yellow Split Pea Flatbread (see page 114) for the rest of the family. This recipe also makes a delicious pasta sauce – blend until smooth and add a little Pumpkin Seed Pesto (see page 121).

SERVES 4 CHILDREN

50g/¼ cup red lentils
1 tsp apple cider vinegar or lemon juice (optional)
1 tbsp coconut or olive oil
1 small red onion, finely chopped
½ celery stick, finely chopped
½ garlic clove, crushed
½ small butternut squash or 1 large parsnip or a mix of both, peeled and cut into 1cm chunks
¼ tsp curry powder
¼ ground coriander
¼ tsp ground turmeric
1 tsp tomato purée
1 × 160g tin coconut cream
1 × 400g tin chopped tomatoes
4 tbsp water or vegetable or chicken stock (homemade or very low salt)

Soak the red lentils overnight in water with the vinegar or lemon juice. This is an optional step that helps the lentils to become more digestible. Drain and rinse in the morning.

Place the oil in a large saucepan over a medium heat. Add the onion and celery and fry for 3–5 minutes, or until soft. Add the garlic and cook for a further minute.

Add the lentils, squash or parsnip, curry powder, coriander and turmeric to the pan, along with the tomato purée, coconut cream and chopped tomatoes. Add 2 tablespoons of water or stock to each empty tin and swirl out any residue into the mixture. Stir, cover wih a lid and bring to the boil.

Reduce the heat and simmer for 20–25 minutes, stirring from time to time so the lentils do not catch on the bottom of the pan, until the squash or parsnip is tender and the lentils are soft. You might need to add a little more water or stock if the sauce gets too thick.

STORAGE

Can be stored in a sealed container in the fridge for 3–4 days, or in the freezer for up to 3 months.

CELERY-FREE
Replace with fennel or leave out.

YELLOW SPLIT PEA FLATBREAD

A perfect 'bread' recipe for vegans and kids who have multiple allergies.
Yellow split peas and tahini are both excellent sources of fibre and protein,
as well as many vitamins and other nutrients. This is a dense flatbread – it will
not rise, but this makes it suitable as a pizza base, too. Serve it with Coconut
& Tomato Lentil Curry (see page 113), one of the dips on pages 56–57,
or alongside a boiled egg as 'soldiers'.

MAKES 8 SLICES

140g yellow split peas,
soaked overnight in
water, then drained
and rinsed
2 tbsp light tahini paste
1 tsp tomato purée
½ garlic clove, crushed
1 tbsp apple cider vinegar
1 tbsp maple syrup or
honey (not for children
under 12 months)
100ml water or vegetable
stock (homemade or
very low salt)
1 tbsp olive oil
½ tsp ground turmeric
½ tsp baking powder

Preheat the oven to 180°C/160°C fan/gas mark 4 and line a
22cm square tin with parchment paper. It does not have to be
a perfect fit – the parchment paper can hang over the sides.

Place all the ingredients in a food processor and blitz until
the mixture is smooth, stopping every now and then to scrape
down the sides. The mixture will end up quite runny. (At this
stage, you could add 1 tablespoon mixed Mediterranean
herbs if you are making it as a pizza base.)

Pour the mixture into the prepared tin, using the back
of a spoon to ensure it is level. Bake in the oven for
20–22 minutes, turning the tray around after 15 minutes.

Remove from the oven and leave to cool and firm up in
the tin for 10 minutes. Turn it out, peel off the parchment
paper and cut into slices.

STORAGE

Best eaten on the day of
baking but can be stored
in a sealed container for
2 days, or in the freezer
for up to 1 month. Defrost
at room temperature and
place in the oven to reheat
before serving.

GLUTEN-FREE
Use gluten-free
baking powder.

SESAME-FREE
Replace tahini
paste with sunflower
seed butter or
cashew butter.

SMOKEY BUTTERBEAN & CASHEW CASSEROLE

This flavoursome casserole is sure to become a staple in your household for everyone to enjoy. Cashew nuts contain the nutrients that help to make the happiness hormone serotonin, as well as vitamin B6, magnesium, niacin and tryptophan. For a stronger smokey flavour, add a little more paprika.

SERVES 4–5 CHILDREN

1 tbsp coconut oil
  or unsalted butter
1 small red onion, chopped
½–1 garlic clove, crushed
50g/½ cup cashew nuts
1 × 400g tin butterbeans,
  rinsed and drained
250g/½ small butternut
  squash, peeled and
  chopped
1 × 160g tin coconut cream
1 tsp apple cider vinegar
½ tsp smoked sweet
  paprika
¼ tsp ground cumin
Pinch of fine sea salt
  (not for children under
  12 months)

Place the coconut oil or butter in a saucepan over a medium heat. Add the onion and fry for 3–5 minutes, or until soft. Add the garlic and cook for a further minute, stirring to ensure it doesn't burn.

Meanwhile, roughly chop the cashews, or whizz them to breadcrumb consistency in a food processor for babies.

Stir the cashews and all the remaining ingredients into the pan. Cover with a lid and bring to the boil. Reduce the heat and simmer for 25–30 minutes, or until the squash is tender.

Serve with steamed green vegetables, whizz to a purée or mash.

STORAGE

Can be stored in a sealed container in the fridge for 3–4 days, or in the freezer for up to 3 months.

NUT-FREE
Use sunflower seeds
instead of cashews.

COCONUT & SUNFLOWER SEED CHICKEN FINGERS

These succulent fingers introduce little ones to a bit of texture with crunchy sunflower seeds and desiccated coconut. Sunflower seeds contain a phospholipid called lecithin, which is a source of choline, important for brain health, memory and learning. Cooking the thigh before cutting into fingers makes the chicken very tender and easier for young children to eat and digest. For babies, cut the chicken into small, bite-sized pieces. Try this coating on firm tofu sticks, if you don't eat meat. Serve with Coconut Yoghurt & Lime Dip (see page 56).

SERVES 2 ADULTS & 1 CHILD

250g/2–3 small boneless, skinless chicken thighs
6 tbsp coconut yoghurt
Zest and juice of 1 lime
3 tbsp sunflower seeds, ground
3 tbsp desiccated coconut
Pinch of fine sea salt (not for children under 12 months)
Drizzle of olive oil

STORAGE

Can be stored in the fridge for 3 days. Freeze the chicken for up to 3 months before adding the sunflower coconut crust. Defrost, then add the crust and bake.

6 MONTHS PLUS

Place the chicken thighs on a board between two pieces of parchment paper. Using a rolling pin, flatten them until they are about 5mm thick.

Mix the yoghurt, lime zest and juice together in a small bowl. Add the chicken thighs, ensuring they get an even coating. Cover and place in the fridge to marinate for at least 30 minutes. (This is an optional step, but it tenderises the chicken and intensifies the flavours.)

Preheat the oven to 180°C/160°C fan/gas mark 4 and line a baking tray with parchment paper.

Mix the ground sunflower seeds, desiccated coconut and salt, if using, on a plate. Wipe down each thigh with some kitchen paper to remove most of the marinade, then coat them with the crumb mix, using your hands to press it on to each side. Place the chicken on the prepared baking tray, drizzle with a little oil, then roast in the oven for 20–25 minutes, or until cooked through and slightly golden.

Remove from the oven and cut into fingers to serve.

CRISPY SWEET POTATO CHIPS

Another finger food that provides a great opportunity for developing fine motor skills. Aromatic turmeric adds colour, flavour and health benefits to these scrumptious chips. Turmeric has been used in cooking and traditional medicine for centuries and is known for its anti-inflammatory and antimicrobial properties.

SERVES 2 ADULTS & 1 CHILD

2 large sweet potatoes, peeled and sliced into 5mm-thick chips
2 tbsp cornflour
2 tbsp olive oil
2 tsp mixed dried Mediterranean herbs
½ tsp ground turmeric
Freshly ground black pepper (optional)
Pinch of fine sea salt (not for children under 12 months)

STORAGE

Freeze once coated in the cornflour and herbs for up to 3 months. Roast from frozen for 35–40 minutes.

Soak the chips in water for 20 minutes. This will help make them crispy on the outside and soft on the inside.

Preheat the oven to 200°C/180°C fan/gas mark 5 and line a baking tray with parchment paper.

Pat the chips dry with kitchen paper.

Place the cornflour in a plastic food bag, add the chips and shake so they get an even coating. Add the olive oil, herbs, turmeric and seasoning, if using, to the bag and shake again.

Place the chips on the prepared baking tray in a single layer, making sure they are not touching each other. Roast in the oven for 30–35 minutes, turning them halfway through.

Remove from the oven and allow to cool slightly before serving.

TIP Top tips for crispy chips:
* Cut them as evenly as possible and not too thin, otherwise they will burn.
* Make sure the starch is absorbed by the cornflour before adding the spices, herbs and oil.
* If you don't have cornflour, use rice flour, tapioca flour or potato flour, or leave out – they just won't be as crispy.
* Make sure you don't overcrowd the tray.
* Only turn the chips once.

LENTIL CHICKEN NUGGETS

A protein-packed nugget which is delicious served with Zesty Lemon & Pesto Dip (see page 56). Swap chicken for cod, salmon or halloumi strips. If you have the time, it's worth making Pumpkin Seed Pesto (see page 121) for a zinc boost, but the recipe works well with shop-bought varieties, too.

SERVES 2 ADULTS & 1 CHILD

250g/2–3 small skinless, boneless chicken thighs
2 slices of stale wholemeal bread or toast, crusts removed, or 6 tbsp Panko breadcrumbs
6 tbsp red lentils, ground to a powder in a food processor or coffee grinder
6 tbsp pesto (ideally Pumpkin Seed Pesto, see page 121)
3 tbsp milk of choice
Drizzle of olive oil

STORAGE

Can be stored in the fridge for 3 days, or in the freezer for up to 3 months. Only freeze before cooking if the chicken was not frozen beforehand – never re-freeze defrosted chicken. Can be reheated straight from frozen.

Preheat the oven to 180°C/160°C fan/gas mark 4 and line a baking tray with parchment paper.

Place the chicken thighs on a board between two pieces of parchment paper. Using a rolling pin, flatten until they are about 5mm thick.

Cut each thigh into 4–5 strips, then cut the strips in half to make nuggets.

Blitz the bread in a food processor to make breadcrumbs.

Set out three plates – place half the ground lentils in the first, mix the pesto and milk in the second, and combine the breadcrumbs and remaining ground lentils in the third. Dip each nugget into the lentils, then pesto and finally into the breadcrumb mixture.

Place the nuggets on the prepared baking tray, ensuring they are not touching each other, and drizzle over a little oil. Roast in the oven for 20–22 minutes, or until cooked through and crispy, turning them after 10 minutes.

GLUTEN-FREE
Use gluten-free bread or ground almonds.

12 MONTHS PLUS

CHEESY MASHED SWEET POTATO

A tasty, filling meal for your baby, or a veggie side for the whole family.

SERVES 2 ADULTS & 1 CHILD

2 medium sweet potatoes,
   peeled and cut into
   large chunks
1 medium white potato,
   peeled and cut into
   large chunks
2 tsp unsalted butter
30g Cheddar, grated
Freshly ground black
   pepper (optional)
Pinch of fine sea salt
   (not for children
   under 12 months)

Place the veg in a saucepan, cover with water and bring to the boil. Reduce the heat and simmer for 10–15 minutes, or until soft.

Drain and return to the pan. Mash thoroughly, then add the butter, cheese and seasoning, if using. Mash again and serve.

STORAGE

Can be stored in the fridge for 3 days, or in the freezer for up to 3 months.

DAIRY-FREE
Replace the butter with dairy-free spread and the cheese with vegan hard cheese.

6 MONTHS PLUS

PUMPKIN SEED PESTO

Stir this nut-free pesto into pasta, fish and chicken dishes, use as a topping for pizzas or a relish in wraps and sandwiches. Pumpkin seeds are little powerhouses that not only improve brain development but also promote sleep. Garlic is a popular remedy for fighting colds, so grab some when your child is under the weather.

SERVES 2–3 CHILDREN

5 tbsp pumpkin seeds
1 tsp apple cider vinegar (optional)
¼ garlic clove, crushed
75g baby spinach
10g fresh basil leaves
25g Parmesan, finely grated (optional)
Juice of ½ lemon
Freshly ground black pepper (optional)
3 tbsp olive oil

STORAGE

Can be stored in an airtight container in the fridge for 3 days, or in ice cube trays in the freezer for up to 3 months.

DAIRY-FREE
Use a hard vegan cheese instead of Parmesan.

If you have time, soak the pumpkin seeds overnight, which activates them to release their zinc, by placing them in a small bowl, covering them with water. Add the apple cider vinegar, if using, and leave overnight. Drain and rinse in the morning.

Preheat the oven to 180°C/160°C fan/gas mark 4.

Transfer the seeds to a baking tray and pat dry with kitchen paper to remove any excess water. Roast for 3 minutes, then turn the seeds and roast for a further 2 minutes. Leave to cool.

Place the cooled seeds in a food processor and blitz until they resemble fine breadcrumbs.

Add the garlic, spinach, basil, Parmesan, lemon juice and pepper, if using, to the processor and continue to blend, stopping every now and again to scrape the sides down.

While the machine is running, add the olive oil, 1 tablespoon at a time, until combined.

TIP Soaking seeds before using them is particularly important for people following a predominantly plant-based diet, as many seeds and grains contain phytates which block zinc absorption.

TAHINI, MUSTARD & TARRAGON CHICKEN THIGHS

A calcium-rich twist on traditional honey and mustard chicken, this is super creamy and delicious. Tahini, normally found in hummus, is made from sesame seeds, which are naturally rich in calcium, magnesium and phosphorus – three of the most important micronutrients needed for healthy bones. Serve with Cheesy Mashed Sweet Potato (see page 120) and steamed green veg.

SERVES 4–5 PEOPLE

6 tsp light tahini paste
6 tsp grainy mustard
6 tsp runny honey or
    maple syrup
Juice of 1 lemon
6 tsp dried tarragon
500g/5–6 chicken thighs

STORAGE

Can be stored in the fridge for 3 days, or in the freezer for up to 3 months.

Preheat the oven to 180°C/160°C fan/gas mark 4.

In a small bowl, combine the tahini, mustard, honey or maple syrup, lemon juice and tarragon. Add the chicken thighs and massage in the marinade. Cover and leave for at least 15 minutes (you could leave them in the fridge all day – the longer the better).

Transfer the chicken to a baking tray and pour the marinade juices over the top. Add the empty lemon halves and 4 tablespoons water to the bottom of the tray to keep the chicken moist and prevent it from sticking. Roast in the oven for 25–30 minutes, or until cooked through.

12
MONTHS
PLUS

MUSTARD-FREE
Swap mustard for
3 tsp horseradish.

SESAME-FREE
Swap tahini for cashew
or almond butter.

CRUNCHY CHICKEN DIPPERS

A healthier version of fried chicken, this will be a hit with fussy eaters who are drawn to crunchy, beige food. It works equally well with tofu or halloumi, for those who don't eat meat. Serve with Rosemary & Garlic Chips (see opposite).

SERVES 2 ADULTS & 1 CHILD

2 slices of stale wholemeal bread or toast, crusts removed, or 6 tbsp Panko breadcrumbs
2 tsp mixed dried Mediterranean herbs
2 tsp smoked paprika
1 tsp ground cumin
Freshly ground black pepper (optional)
Pinch of fine sea salt (not for children under 12 months)
25g spelt, wholemeal or chickpea (gram) flour
1 egg, lightly beaten
250g boneless, skinless chicken (2 breasts or 4 thighs), sliced into 1cm strips
2 tbsp olive oil

Tear the bread into a few pieces and blitz in a food processor with the herbs, spices and seasoning, if using. No need to blitz Panko breadcrumbs.

Set out three plates – the first for the flour, the second for the egg and the third for the breadcrumb mixture. Dip the chicken strips into the flour, then the egg and finally into the breadcrumbs, making sure they are evenly coated.

Place a large frying pan over a medium heat, add the oil and leave until it is sizzling.

Using tongs, carefully place the chicken strips in the pan and fry them for a few minutes on all sides, or until they are cooked through and the batter is crispy and slightly browned – depending on the thickness of the strips, this should take 8–12 minutes. You could also bake them in the oven with chips (see opposite) for 20–25 minutes, turning once.

STORAGE

Can be stored in the fridge for 3 days, or in the freezer for up to 3 months. Reheat straight from frozen.

GLUTEN-FREE
Use gluten-free bread and flour.

EGG-FREE
Swap egg for 1 tbsp milk or coconut milk.

ROSEMARY & GARLIC CHIPS

6 MONTHS PLUS

Kids love chips! And why not? Potatoes contain a lot of goodness, and cooked here with garlic and rosemary, they are supercharged with herbs that help boost immunity and concentration.

SERVES 2 ADULTS & 1 CHILD

3 medium white potatoes, skin on, washed and cut into chips
2 tbsp olive oil
Large sprig of rosemary, leaves finely chopped, or 2 tsp dried
Pinch of fine sea salt (not for children under 12 months)
1 garlic clove, finely chopped

STORAGE

Can be stored in the fridge for 3 days, or in the freezer for up to 3 months. Reheat from frozen.

Preheat the oven to 220°C/200°C fan/gas mark 7.

Soak the chips in a saucepan of cold water for 5–10 minutes, then place over a high heat. Bring to the boil and cook for 3 minutes. Drain and pat the chips dry with kitchen paper.

Transfer to a baking tray and toss in the oil.

Lay the chips out in a single layer across the tray, ensuring they are not touching each other. Sprinkle the rosemary and salt, if using, over the chips and bake in the oven for 35 minutes, shaking every 10 minutes, so they crisp up evenly. Halfway through the cooking time, scatter over the garlic.

SUPERCHARGED BEEF & LENTIL RAGU WITH SPAGHETTI

This ragu is made the Italian way, with chicken livers to boost the iron and give a richer taste. The lentils disappear into the sauce, so kids won't even notice they're getting the extra protein and fibre. We make large batches and store it in the freezer. Swap the beef and liver for soya mince, for those who don't eat meat. Avoid eating liver when you are pregnant.

SERVES 5–6 PEOPLE

2 tbsp olive oil
1 small onion, diced
2 garlic cloves, crushed
400–500g beef mince
2 chicken livers, diced, or
    1 tbsp Sage & Cranberry
    Chicken Liver Pâté
    (see page 103)
½ celery stick, diced
1 carrot, peeled and
    finely grated
½ courgette, finely grated
1 red pepper, deseeded
    and diced
3 tbsp tomato purée
1 × 400g tin tomatoes
1 × 400g tin green lentils,
    rinsed and drained
Handful of fresh basil
    leaves, plus extra
    to serve
1 tsp freshly grated
    nutmeg
1–2 tbsp balsamic vinegar
Freshly ground black
    pepper (optional)
Pinch of fine sea salt
Spaghetti (30–40g per child
    and 70–80g per adult)
20g grated Cheddar or
    Parmesan, grated

Heat the oil in a large saucepan over a low to medium heat. Add the onion and fry for 3–5 minutes, or until soft and translucent. Add the garlic and cook for a further minute.

Increase the heat and add the beef, stirring frequently to brown it all over.

Reduce the heat and stir in all the remaining ingredients, except the spaghetti and cheese. Bring to a boil, then reduce the heat again, cover with a lid and leave the ragu to simmer for at least 40 minutes, or until everything is soft and a rich red colour.

Meanwhile, cook the spaghetti according to the packet instructions. Drain and return to the pan.

Stir the ragu sauce into the pasta and sprinkle over some basil leaves and a little Cheddar or Parmesan, to serve.

DAIRY-FREE
Use a hard vegan cheese instead of Cheddar or Parmesan.

GLUTEN-FREE
Use gluten-free spaghetti.

CELERY-FREE
Replace with fennel or leave out.

STORAGE
Can be stored in a sealed container in the fridge for 3 days, or in the freezer for up to 3 months.

MINI CHRISTMAS BURGERS

Turkey and chestnuts make a delicious combo. What's more, the tryptophan
in turkey promotes a good night's sleep – a bonus for all the family. Turkey
is a lean meat, so I have added a little bit of sausage meat to make the
burgers nice and moist.

MAKES 10–12 MINI BURGERS

40g dried apricots
(ideally unsulphured)
2 tbsp olive or coconut oil
1 small red onion, diced
½ garlic clove, crushed
1 small apple, peeled,
cored and finely grated
200g turkey mince
100g sausage meat
25g/¼ cup porridge oats
50g/⅓ cup chestnuts,
finely chopped
1 tsp tomato purée
Zest of 1 orange
1 free-range egg yolk
Freshly ground black
pepper (optional)
Pinch of fine sea salt

STORAGE

Can be stored in the
fridge for 24 hours,
or frozen after cooking
for up to 2 months.

Place the apricots in a small bowl and pour boiling water over
the top. Leave to soak for 5 minutes, then drain and finely chop.

Place 1 tablespoon of the oil in a small frying pan over a
medium heat. Add the onion and fry for 3–5 minutes, or until
soft. Add the garlic and cook for a further minute. Leave to cool.

Meanwhile, squeeze any excess liquid from the grated apple.
Place the apple in a large bowl with the apricots, garlic and
onion. Add the turkey, sausage meat, oats, chestnuts, tomato
purée, orange zest, egg and seasoning, if using. Mix well and
use your hands to shape the mixture into little balls, then
flatten them slightly to make small burgers. Place them
on a plate, cover and refrigerate for 1 hour to firm them up.

Preheat the oven to 180°C/160°C fan/gas mark 4.

Place an ovenproof frying pan over a medium heat and add
the remaining oil. Sear the burgers for 2 minutes on each side
– this will prevent them from falling apart – then transfer to
the oven and cook for 15 minutes, turning halfway through.

Leave to cool slightly before serving in mini wholemeal buns.

NUT-FREE
Omit chestnuts.

EGG-FREE
Omit egg yolk and
increase chilling time
(egg helps to bind
the mixture).

MINTY LAMB KOFTAS

Lamb is an excellent source of complete protein, containing all the
essential amino acids. Serve these with Kefir Flatbreads (see page 132),
Tomato Relish (see page 134) and some Avocado Mayo (see page 133)
for a Mediterranean treat that offers a healthier twist on lamb kebabs.
A perfect family meal for the weekend.

MAKES 14 MINI KOFTAS

2 tbsp olive oil
2 small shallots or ½
    onion, finely chopped
1 garlic clove, crushed
350g lamb mince
6 mint leaves, finely
    chopped, or 2 heaped
    tsp dried
Freshly ground black
    pepper (optional)
Pinch of fine sea salt
    (not for children
    under 12 months)

STORAGE

Can be stored in the
fridge for 24 hours, or
frozen before cooking
for up to 3 months.

6
MONTHS
PLUS

Place 1 tablespoon of the oil in a small frying pan over
a medium heat. Add the shallots or onion and fry for
3–5 minutes, or until soft. Add the garlic and cook
for a further minute.

Tip the onion mixture into a bowl and add the lamb mince,
mint and seasoning, if using. Mix well and use your hands
to shape the mixture into small balls, then flatten them
slightly to make mini koftas.

Place a large frying pan over a medium heat and add the
remaining oil. Add the koftas and fry for a 5–6 minutes
on each side, turning them carefully, until they are
brown and cooked through.

KEFIR FLATBREADS

This is super-healthy bread that is gentle on little tummies and simple to make. Kefir helps to bind the oat flour to make an easy-to-manage dough.

MAKES 4 LARGE OR 8 MINI FLATBREADS

200g/2 cups porridge oats, plus extra for dusting
2 heaped tsp flax seeds
240ml/1 cup kefir or natural yoghurt
1½ tsp baking powder
Pinch of fine sea salt (not for children under 12 months)

STORAGE

Once cooked, these can be stored in the fridge for 3 days, or in the freezer for up to 3 months. Best reheated to serve.

6 MONTHS PLUS

Blitz the oats and flax seeds in a food processor with a grinding blade until you have a flour-like consistency.

Tip them into a bowl, add the kefir, baking powder and salt, if using, and bring together to make a dough. Cover in a beeswax wrap or clingfilm and place in the fridge for 15 minutes.

Divide the dough into 4–8 pieces.

Place the dough on some parchment paper and press into thin pitta bread shapes. You can place a second sheet of parchment paper on top and roll with a rolling pin, if you want them nice and thin.

Place a frying or griddle pan over a high heat and toast the flatbreads one at a time for about 2 minutes on each side. Keep them warm by storing in a tea towel until ready to serve.

GLUTEN-FREE
Use gluten-free oats and baking powder.

DAIRY-FREE
Replace kefir with coconut yoghurt.

AVOCADO MAYO

Chives and parsley give this mayo a fresh taste that kids will love.
Avocados are great for the skin and also help to boost the gut microbiome.

2 free-range egg yolks
1 tsp Dijon mustard
1 tbsp red wine vinegar
40ml avocado oil
120ml/½ cup light olive oil
2–3 chives, finely chopped
Large sprig of parsley,
    leaves finely chopped
Freshly ground black
    pepper (optional)
Pinch of fine sea salt
    (not for children
    under 12 months)

Use an electric whisk or hand blender to blitz the egg yolks, mustard and vinegar together in a bowl or jug.

Combine the two oils in a small jug and pour them into the egg mixture, drip by drip, whisking all the time, until it becomes thick and creamy.

Stir in the chives, parsley and seasoning, if using, to serve.

STORAGE

Can be stored in the fridge for up to 7 days. Not suitable for freezing.

MUSTARD-FREE
Replace with
½ tsp horseradish,
or leave out.

EGG-FREE
Swap egg yolks for
120ml soya milk.

6 MONTHS PLUS

AS LONG AS THE
EGGS HAVE A
RED LION STAMP
ON THEM

TOMATO RELISH

This versatile sauce can be used on pizzas, as a salsa to serve with meatballs or burgers, or as a filling for baked potatoes or quesadillas.

SERVES 4–5 CHILDREN

1 tbsp olive oil
1 onion, roughly chopped
1 garlic clove, crushed
1 ×400g tin chopped
    tomatoes
1 tbsp balsamic vinegar or
    apple balsamic vinegar
2 tsp Worcestershire
    sauce
1 tsp maple syrup or honey
1 tsp fresh or dried
    oregano
Freshly ground black
    pepper (optional)
Pinch of fine sea salt

Place the oil in a saucepan over a medium heat. Add the onion and fry for 3–5 minutes, or until soft and translucent. Add the garlic and cook for a further minute.

Stir in the remaining ingredients, bring to the boil and cook for 2–3 minutes.

Season, if using, then reduce the heat, cover with a lid and leave to simmer for at least 10 minutes.

Remove from the heat and blitz briefly with a hand blender. Return the pan to the heat and leave to simmer uncovered until it is nice and thick.

STORAGE

Can be stored in a sealed container in the fridge for 3 weeks, or in the freezer for up to 3 months.

GLUTEN-FREE
Use Biona
Worcester Sauce.

12
MONTHS
PLUS

BEEFY QUINOA & BEETROOT BURGERS

This is a great way to use up leftover quinoa. Swap the beef for puy lentils,
if you don't eat meat. Serve with Crispy Sweet Potato Chips
(see page 117) and steamed veg.

MAKES 8 MINI BURGERS

45g white or red quinoa
(135g cooked weight)
120ml/½ cup water or
vegetable or chicken
stock (homemade or
very low salt)
2 tbsp olive or coconut oil
1 small red onion, diced
1 garlic clove, crushed
1 medium cooked
beetroot, peeled
250g beef mince
1 tsp tomato purée
Sprig of rosemary,
leaves finely chopped,
or 1 tsp dried
Freshly ground black
pepper (optional)
Pinch of fine sea salt
(not for children
under 12 months)

STORAGE

Can be stored in the
fridge for 24 hours, or
freeze after cooking and
keep for up to 2 months.

If you are using uncooked quinoa, rinse and place it in a pan
with the water or stock. Cover with a lid and bring to the boil.
Reduce the heat and simmer for 15 minutes, or until the liquid
is absorbed and the quinoa is cooked. Remove from the heat
and leave the lid on for 5 minutes to allow it to fluff up.
Then remove the lid and leave to cool.

Place 1 tablespoon of the oil in a small frying pan over a
medium heat. Add the onion and fry for 3–5 minutes, or until
soft. Add the garlic and cook for a further minute. Leave to cool.

Grate the beetroot or cut it into chunks and whizz in a food
processor. Squeeze out any excess juice, then transfer the
beetroot to a large bowl. Add the cooked quinoa, onion, garlic,
beef mince, tomato purée, rosemary and seasoning, if using.
Mix well and use your hands to shape the mixture into little
balls, then flatten them slightly to make burgers. Place them
on a plate, cover and refrigerate for 20 minutes to firm up.

Preheat the oven to 180°C/160°C fan/gas mark 4.

Place an ovenproof frying pan over a medium heat and add
the remaining oil. Sear the burgers for 2 minutes on each side
– this will prevent them from falling apart – then transfer to
the oven and cook for 10 minutes, turning halfway through.
The beetroot will burn easily, so watch them closely.

Leave to cool slightly before serving.

BARLEY & PEA RISOTTO

6 MONTHS PLUS

Let the oven do the work! This baked risotto eliminates the need for standing over the hob ladling in stock. Busy parents can get a second meal out of this by using leftovers to make arancini (see page 138).

SERVES 4–5 CHILDREN

1 tbsp unsalted butter
   or olive oil
2 shallots or 1 small
   onion, diced
½–1 garlic clove, crushed
150g/1 cup pearled barley
1 bay leaf
500ml/2 cups chicken
   or vegetable stock
   (homemade or very
   low salt)
100g asparagus
20g Parmesan,
   finely grated
3–4 chives, finely chopped
Freshly ground black
   pepper (optional)
Pinch of fine sea salt
   (not for children
   under 12 months)

Pea purée
180g/1 cup frozen peas
1 tbsp finely chopped
   mint leaves
Juice of ½ lemon
2 tbsp olive oil

STORAGE

Can be stored in a sealed container in the fridge for 3 days, or in the freezer for up to 3 months.

Preheat the oven to 180°C/160°C fan/gas mark 4.

Place the butter or oil in a lidded flameproof casserole dish over a medium heat. Add the shallots or onions and fry for 3–4 minutes, or until soft. Add the garlic and cook for a further minute.

Stir in the pearled barley and bay leaf and cook for 1–2 minutes. Pour in the stock, bring to the boil and cover with a tightly fitting lid. Transfer to the oven for 35–40 minutes, or until the barley is soft, but still has a slight bite.

Meanwhile, make the pea purée. Place the frozen peas in a bowl and pour over some boiling water to defrost them. Drain and transfer 100g peas to a jug. Add the mint, lemon juice and olive oil and blend using a hand blender until smooth.

Steam the asparagus and either chop it finely or leave whole to serve on the side. (If you are planning to make arancini with any leftover risotto, serve the asparagus on the side.)

Drain away any excess liquid from the risotto and remove the bay leaf. Gently stir in the pea purée, the remaining whole peas, the Parmesan, chives, seasoning and the steamed asparagus.

DAIRY-FREE
Use a hard vegan cheese.

GLUTEN-FREE
Swap the pearled barley for risotto rice.

BARLEY & PEA ARANCINI

These arancini are perfect for baby-led weaning, especially if your baby doesn't like eating off a spoon. Panko breadcrumbs give the best results, but you could try making your own by blitzing two slices of wholemeal bread in a food processor.

MAKES 8–10 BALLS

6 tbsp Panko breadcrumbs
Drizzle of olive oil
300g/2 cups Barley & Pea Risotto (see page 137)
1 ball of mozzarella, cut into 1cm cubes
4 tbsp spelt or wholemeal flour
1 tbsp fresh oregano leaves or 1 tsp dried
1 free-range egg, beaten
Zest of ½ lemon

STORAGE

Can be stored in a sealed container in the fridge for up to 3 days.

Preheat the oven to 180°C/160°C fan/gas mark 4 and line a baking tray with parchment paper.

Place the breadcrumbs on the baking tray, drizzle with a little olive oil and transfer to the oven for 3–5 minutes. (This is an optional step, but the toasted breadcrumbs give the arancini a lovely golden look.)

To form the arancini, scoop a walnut-sized portion of risotto into your hands. Place a mozzarella cube into the centre and wrap the risotto around it to seal completely. Repeat until you have used up all the risotto.

Prepare three small bowls – the first with the flour and oregano, the second with the beaten egg, and the third with the breadcrumbs and lemon zest. Dip each ball into the flour, shaking off any excess, then into the egg and finally into the breadcrumb mixture. Ensure the arancini are evenly coated.

Place on the prepared baking tray, drizzle with a little olive oil and bake for 20 minutes. Once cooked, let them sit for a couple of minutes before removing from the tray and serving. Best served warm so the cheese is melty inside.

DAIRY-FREE
Use a hard vegan cheese instead of Parmesan and a vegan mozzarella-style cheese. Or stuff the arancini with finely chopped meat or green herbs.

EGG-FREE
Use 2 tbsp psyllium husks and 6 tbsp water instead.

GLUTEN-FREE
Swap the pearled barley for risotto rice (cooked rice can only be kept in the fridge for up to 24 hours). Use gluten-free flour instead of spelt and breadcrumbs made from gluten-free bread.

CREAMY RED PEPPER & FLAGEOLET BEAN RISOTTO

6 MONTHS PLUS

A yummy risotto with Mediterranean vegetables that makes a great family meal.

SERVES 4-5 CHILDREN

190g/1 cup risotto rice
Knob of unsalted butter
2 tbsp olive oil
1 small red onion, diced
1 garlic clove, crushed
500ml/2 cups hot chicken
or vegetable stock
(homemade or
very low salt)
1 red pepper, deseeded
and diced
1 small courgette, diced
1 × 400g tin flageolet
beans, rinsed
and drained
3–4 fresh sage leaves,
finely chopped, or
1 heaped tsp dried
½ tsp freshly
grated nutmeg
25ml cream or milk
of choice
25g Cheddar, grated
25g Parmesan, grated
Freshly ground black
pepper (optional)
Pinch of fine sea salt
(not for children
under 12 months)

Soak the rice and wash thoroughly to remove any impurities.

Place the butter and oil in a large saucepan over a medium heat. Add the onion and fry for 3–5 minutes, or until soft. Add the garlic and cook for a further minute.

Drain the rice then stir into the pan. Add one ladleful of stock and stir every minute or so, until the rice has absorbed it.

Add the red pepper, courgette, flageolet beans, sage and nutmeg, followed by another ladleful of stock, stirring all the time. Keep on adding stock and stirring until the rice is lovely and soft. This should take about 25 minutes.

Just before serving, stir in the cream or milk, the cheeses and seasoning, if using.

DAIRY-FREE
Swap butter for dairy-free spread or oil, Cheddar for a hard vegan cheese, and use 1–2 heaped tsp nutritional yeast instead of Parmesan.

STORAGE

Can be stored in a sealed container in the fridge for up to 24 hours. Does not freeze well.

ASIAN PRAWN FRIED RICE

A quick store-cupboard and freezer meal that the whole family can enjoy. Replace the prawns with firm tofu for vegetarians and vegans.

SERVES 2 ADULTS & 1 CHILD

190g/1 cup brown rice
200g frozen petits pois
1 tbsp sesame oil
3 spring onions,
    finely sliced
2 peppers, deseeded
    and finely sliced
1 star anise pod
Small knob of fresh
    root ginger, peeled
    and grated
150g frozen cooked
    prawns, defrosted
30g/¼ cup sunflower
    seeds
2 tbsp tamari or light
    soya sauce
Squeeze of fresh
    lime juice

Soak the rice and wash thoroughly to remove any impurities. Place in a pan of boiling water and cook for 20–25 minutes, or until tender. Drain and set aside.

Place the petits pois in a bowl and pour some boiling water over the top to defrost them.

Meanwhile, place the sesame oil in a large frying pan over a medium heat. Add the spring onions and fry for 3 minutes.

Add the peppers, star anise and ginger and fry for 3 minutes, before adding the prawns, drained petits pois, sunflower seeds, tamari or soya, lime juice and cooked rice. Stir well to heat through and serve.

STORAGE

Can be stored in a sealed container in the fridge for up to 24 hours. Only reheat once. Does not freeze well.

GLUTEN-FREE
Use gluten-free
soya sauce.

SESAME-FREE
Use olive or
rapeseed oil.

SMOKEY PRAWN & PEA PAELLA

Paella is a great one-pot supper and a super-tasty way to get kids to eat lots of different coloured vegetables. You can make this completely plant-based by swapping the chicken for firm tofu, the prawns for chickpeas, using veg stock and adding some extra paprika instead of the chorizo.

SERVES 2 ADULTS & 1 CHILD

190g/1 cup paella
   or risotto rice
1 tbsp olive oil
1 small red onion,
   finely sliced
1 garlic clove, crushed
50g mild chorizo
   sausage, diced
2 tsp smoked paprika
2 saffron strands, soaked
   in a splash of warm
   water for a few minutes
250ml/1 cup passata
175g/1 chicken breast,
   cut into 1cm pieces
125g mixed peppers,
   deseeded and
   finely sliced
500ml/2 cups hot chicken
   stock (homemade or
   very low salt)
100g frozen cooked
   prawns, defrosted
75g frozen petits pois
Juice of ½ lemon
1 tbsp chopped parsley
Freshly ground black
   pepper (optional)
Few chilli flakes (adults
   and older kids only)

Soak the rice and wash thoroughly to remove any impurities.

Place the oil in a large heavy-based frying pan over a medium heat. Add the onion and fry for 3–5 minutes, or until soft. Add the garlic and cook for a further minute.

Drain the rice, then stir into the pan with the chorizo, paprika and saffron with its soaking liquid. Pour in half the passata and stir again until the liquid is absorbed. Add the remaining passata, as well as the chicken and peppers.

Add a small ladleful of stock every few minutes, stirring often, until the rice softens (this should take about 25 minutes).

Stir in the prawns, petits pois, lemon juice, parsley and pepper, if using. If you like a bit of spice, add a few chilli flakes. Stir well to heat through and serve.

SHELLFISH-FREE
Use diced cod instead
of prawns.

STORAGE

Can be stored in a
sealed container in the
fridge for up to 24 hours.
Only reheat once. Does
not freeze well.

MINI SARDINE & SWEETCORN QUICHES

Sardines are rich in omega 3 fatty acids, which are not only beneficial for infant brain development but also for the immune system. These delicious little quiches can be served at breakfast, lunch or tea.

MAKES 6 MINI QUICHES

1 tbsp olive oil, plus extra for greasing
4 tbsp frozen sweetcorn
1 sweet potato, peeled and coarsely grated
15g Panko or homemade wholemeal breadcrumbs
1 tbsp mixed dried Mediterranean herbs
4 free-range eggs
2 tbsp cream or milk of choice
Freshly ground black pepper (optional)
1 × 200g tin sardines, drained
2 spring onions, finely chopped
1 tsp finely chopped fresh parsley

Preheat the oven to 180°C/160°C fan/gas mark 4 and grease six holes of a deep muffin tin.

Place the sweetcorn in a bowl and pour some boiling water over the top to defrost them. Drain and set aside.

Squeeze the excess liquid out of the grated sweet potato, then place in a bowl with the breadcrumbs, olive oil and herbs, and stir to combine.

Divide the mixture between the muffin holes, pressing down and pushing up the sides a little. Bake in the oven for 10–12 minutes, or until the crust starts to turn golden.

Meanwhile, in a small bowl, beat together the eggs, cream or milk and black pepper, if using.

Mash the sardines in a separate bowl, then stir in the spring onions, sweetcorn and parsley.

Divide the sardine mixture between the muffin holes, then pour the egg and cream mixture on top. Bake for 4–5 minutes, or until the tops are golden and springy to touch.

Leave for a few minutes to firm up before removing them gently with a spatula.

STORAGE

Can be stored in a sealed container in the fridge for 3 days, or in the freezer for up to 3 months.

6 MONTHS PLUS

GLUTEN-FREE
Use gluten-free breadcrumbs.

SALMON & COD POTATO FISH CAKES

For this versatile recipe you can combine any fish – salmon, cod, mackerel and even crab works well. It's important to include oily fish in your baby's diet two to three times a week, as it's high in the fatty acids that are crucial for brain and visual development. I have added a hard-boiled egg to provide some extra protein and choline. These are great served with Lemon & Dill Dip (see page 57).

MAKES 8 MINI FISH CAKES

200g white potatoes, peeled and cut into chunks
70g/½ salmon fillet, skin removed
70g/½ cod fillet, skin removed
4 medium broccoli florets
1 hard-boiled egg, finely chopped
1 tsp horseradish cream or mayonnaise
1 spring onion, chopped
Zest of ½ lemon and 1 tsp lemon juice
1 tsp chopped fresh dill
3–4 chives, chopped
1 tsp unsalted butter or olive oil
Freshly ground black pepper (optional)

STORAGE

Can be stored in the fridge for 2 days, or frozen before or after cooking and kept in the freezer for up to 3 months. Cook through or reheat in the oven once defrosted.

Place the potatoes in a saucepan, cover with water and bring to the boil. Reduce the heat, cover with a lid and cook for 12–15 minutes, or until soft. Drain and leave to steam-dry, then mash.

Steam the fish for 3 minutes and set aside to cool.

Steam the broccoli for 4–5 minutes. Once cooled, chop into small pieces.

Mash the hard-boiled egg in a medium bowl with the horseradish cream or mayonnaise. Flake the fish into the bowl and add the mashed potato, broccoli, spring onion, lemon zest and juice, dill and chives. Mix well to ensure everything is combined. Using clean hands, form 8 mini fish cakes and place them on a plate. Cover and chill in the fridge for 15 minutes.

Place the butter or oil in a frying pan over a medium heat. Once hot, carefully add the fish cakes and seal for 2–3 minutes on each side, until golden and warm through – they don't need any further cooking.

EGG-FREE
Omit hard-boiled egg.

PESTO FISH BITES

This is a super-quick and simple way to serve fish that your kids will love.

1 cod, hake or salmon
fillet, skin removed
2 tbsp Pumpkin Seed
Pesto (see page 121)
or shop-bought pesto
1 tbsp olive oil

STORAGE

Can be stored in the
fridge for up to 24 hours.
Only reheat once. Does
not freeze well.

Preheat the oven to 180°C/160°C fan/gas mark 4 and line
a baking tray with parchment paper.

Pat the fish dry with kitchen paper and slice into 2cm cubes.

Place in a small bowl and add the pesto, ensuring each cube
gets an even coating.

Transfer to the baking tray, drizzle with the olive oil
and bake for 7–10 minutes, or until cooked through.

Remove from the oven and leave to cool slightly
before serving.

ALLERGEN SWAPS
None needed if you
use the Pumpkin Seed
Pesto, rather than
shop-bought.

SALMON COUSCOUS BURGERS

The sweet-spicy combo of ginger and honey makes a perfect
accompaniment for salmon. Serve with peas and carrot batons.

MAKES 8 MINI BURGERS

50g/⅓ cup couscous
(120g/1 cup cooked
weight)

85ml/⅓ cup hot fish,
chicken or vegetable
stock (homemade
or very low salt)

2 tbsp olive oil

½ red onion, diced

1 small carrot, peeled
and grated

70g/½ small salmon
fillet, cut into chunks

Small knob of fresh root
ginger, peeled and
finely grated

Zest of 1 small lemon

1 tsp chopped fresh dill,
or dried

1 tsp maple syrup or honey

1 free-range egg yolk
(optional)

Preheat the oven to 180°C/160°C fan/gas mark 4 and line
a baking tray with parchment paper.

If using uncooked couscous, place in a bowl, pour over the
hot stock, cover and leave to cool.

Meanwhile, place 1 tablespoon of the oil in a small frying pan
over a medium heat. Add the onion and fry for 3–5 minutes,
or until soft.

Squeeze out any excess juice from the carrot and pat the
salmon dry with kitchen paper.

Place the cooked couscous, onion, carrot, salmon, ginger,
lemon zest, dill and maple syrup or honey in a food processor
and blitz until they are well combined. Add the egg yolk, if
using, and blend for a further 3 seconds.

Wash your hands and leave them slightly damp to roll the
mixture into 8 small balls. Place on the prepared baking tray,
flatten them slightly and brush each one with a little olive oil.
Bake in the oven for 12–13 minutes, turning them halfway
through, until slightly golden.

STORAGE

Can be stored in the
fridge for up to 24 hours,
or frozen once cooked for
up to 2 months. Reheat in
the oven once defrosted.

12 MONTHS PLUS

GLUTEN-FREE
Use gluten-free
couscous or quinoa.

EGG-FREE
Omit egg and leave
the mixture in the fridge
for 15 minutes to bind
before baking.

CARROT & APRICOT FALAFELS

These falafels are perfect for a picnic as they are delicious hot or cold.
Serve with Tahini & Herb Dip (see page 57).

MAKES 10 FALAFELS

5 dried apricots
(ideally unsulphured)
1 × 400g tin chickpeas,
rinsed and drained
1 large carrot, peeled
and finely grated
2 tbsp porridge oats
1 tbsp finely chopped
mint leaves
½ garlic clove, crushed
Juice of ½ lemon
1 tsp light tahini paste
½ tsp ground cumin
½ tsp baking powder
1 tbsp olive oil, plus
extra to glaze
Chickpea (gram) or
wholemeal flour,
for dusting

STORAGE

Can be stored in the fridge
for 2 days, or in the freezer
for up to 2 months. Freeze
individually on a lined
baking sheet, then place
in a container. Defrost at
room temperature and
reheat before serving.

Place the apricots in a small bowl and pour boiling water over
the top. Leave to soak for 5 minutes, then drain and finely chop.

Blend the chickpeas in a food processor to a chunky paste.

Squeeze out any excess juice from the carrot, then add to
the food processor, along with the apricots, oats, mint, garlic,
lemon juice, tahini, cumin, baking powder and olive oil. Blitz
until everything is well combined. You will have to stop every
now and then to scrape down the sides.

Lightly flour your hands and scoop out walnut-sized balls
of the mixture. Flatten them slightly, place on the prepared
baking tray and brush with a little olive oil. Repeat until
all the mixture has been used up. Cover the falafels and
refrigerate for 15–30 minutes to firm up.

Preheat the oven to 180°C/160°C fan/gas mark 4 and line
a baking tray with parchment paper.

Bake for 20 minutes, turning them carefully halfway through.

Leave to cool slightly before serving.

GLUTEN-FREE
Use gluten-free oats
and baking powder.

SESAME-FREE
Swap tahini paste
for cashew butter or
sunflower seed butter,
or leave out.

BEAN & CHEESE QUESADILLA

A real crowd pleaser, this is such an easy lunch or supper to rustle up –
plant-based, so it suits everyone, and packed with iron from the black beans.

SERVES 1 ADULT & 1 CHILD

1 tbsp olive oil
¼ red onion,
    finely chopped
1 red pepper, deseeded
    and finely sliced
2 tbsp tomato purée
½ tsp smoked paprika
½ tsp ground cumin
½ tsp ground coriander
1 × 400g tin black beans,
    rinsed and drained
160g frozen or tinned
    sweetcorn, defrosted,
    if necessary, and drained
2 wholemeal or
    seeded wraps
20g Cheddar, grated
½ avocado, peeled,
    stoned and mashed
Squeeze of fresh lime juice

Place the oil in a small saucepan over a low to medium
heat. Add the onion and fry for 3–5 minutes, or until soft.

Stir in the red pepper, tomato purée, paprika, cumin
and coriander and cook for 3 minutes.

Add the black beans and sweetcorn and cook for another
3 minutes. Set aside.

Place a large frying pan over a medium heat and lay a wrap
across the bottom. Dollop the bean mixture on to the wrap
and spread it evenly so it reaches the edges. Sprinkle on
the grated cheese and dot with the mashed avocado.
Cover with the second wrap.

After about 2 minutes, when the bottom wrap is a little crispy,
flip the quesadilla over. Continue to cook on the other side.

Once the cheese in the middle has melted, carefully transfer
the quesadilla to a chopping board and cut into 6 pieces.
Serve warm.

STORAGE

The bean mixture can
be stored in a sealed
container in the fridge
for 3 days, or in the
freezer for up to
3 months.

GLUTEN-FREE
Use gluten-free wraps.

DAIRY-FREE
Use a hard
vegan cheese.

12
MONTHS
PLUS

SWEETCORN CHICKPEA PANCAKES

These savoury pancakes introduce Indian spices without a fiery kick.
They're completely plant-based, with lots of protein and iron.

MAKES 12 PANCAKES

3 tbsp frozen sweetcorn
125g chickpea (gram) flour
250ml/1 cup water
2 spring onions,
    finely chopped
¼ red pepper,
    deseeded and diced
1 tsp ground cumin
1 tsp ground coriander
1 tsp ground turmeric
Freshly ground black
    pepper (optional)
Few chilli flakes (adults
    and older kids only)
Pinch of fine sea salt
    (not for children
    under 12 months)
1 tbsp olive oil

STORAGE

The pancakes can be
stored in the fridge for 2
days, or in the freezer for
up to 3 months. Reheat in
the oven or a frying pan.

Place the sweetcorn in a bowl and pour some boiling water
over the top to defrost them. Drain and tip into a large bowl.

Add all the other ingredients, except the oil, and mix well.
Leave for 10–15 minutes for the flavours to infuse.

Place a heavy-based frying pan over a medium heat and add
a little oil. Using a small ice-cream scoop, pour in 3 small
amounts of batter. Once you can see bubbles forming on
the surface, flip the pancakes over and cook on the other
side for a minute or so.

Add more oil and repeat until you have used up all the batter.

TIP See page 87 to find out how to make your own chickpea flour.

12 MONTHS PLUS

SPELT & COURGETTE MINI PIZZAS

Even though this pizza dough takes time to prepare, it freezes well, so you can always make a large batch to store for a rainy day. The ground seeds added to the dough provide a big mineral and vitamin boost.

MAKES 6 MINI PIZZAS

2 tsp flax seeds
1 tsp chia seeds
1 tbsp sunflower seeds
3.5g/½ sachet dried yeast
200g spelt flour, plus
    extra for dusting
½ tsp runny honey
½ tsp fine sea salt
½ tbsp olive oil, plus
    extra for greasing
125ml/1 ½ cups
    lukewarm water
¼ courgette, grated
1 × portion Tomato Relish
    (see page 134)
200–250g mozzarella
    or Cheddar, grated

STORAGE

The dough can be stored in the fridge for 3–4 days, or in the freezer for up to 3 months. Freeze individual pizzas in beeswax wraps or clingfilm. They defrost in a couple of hours.

GLUTEN-FREE
Use gluten-free bread flour and add 2 tsp gluten-free baking powder, ¼ tsp ground turmeric and 1 heaped tsp xanthan gum.

Blitz the seeds in a food processor with a grinding blade until you have a flour-like consistency.

Place the yeast, spelt flour, honey and salt in a large bowl. Combine the oil and water in a small jug, then slowly add to the dry ingredients until you have a dough that holds together.

Knead on a lightly floured surface for about 5 minutes, or until the dough is smooth and elastic.

Place the dough in a lightly oiled bowl and turn it over so it is completely coated. Cover and leave in a warm place to rise for about 1½ hours, or until tripled in size.

Once the dough has risen, add the courgette and ground seeds and knead to combine. Cover and leave for 30 minutes.

Knock the air out of the dough and return it to the bowl for a final 30 minutes.

Preheat the oven to 220°C/200°C fan/gas mark 7 and place a pizza stone or baking tray in the oven to heat up.

Divide the mixture into six and roll into balls. Using a lightly floured rolling pin and surface, roll out each ball until about 2mm thick. Spread each pizza with a layer of Tomato Relish, followed by a generous amount of grated mozzarella or Cheddar. You can be as creative as you like with extra toppings!

Transfer to the pizza stone or baking tray and bake in the oven for 8–10 minutes, or until the base is crunchy and the cheese is melted and golden brown.

DAIRY-FREE
Use vegan mozzarella-style cheese.

MINI VEGGIE ROSTI

These are perfect for on-the-move weaning and savoury toddler snacks. They make very little mess and can be eaten cold or warm. It's important for little ones to experience different textures, so I've combined a crunchy rosti bottom with a smooth quiche-like topping.

MAKES 6 ROSTI

Olive oil, for greasing
2 tbsp unsalted butter
1 medium baking
  potato, peeled and
  coarsely grated
½ red pepper,
  deseeded and diced
¼ leek, trimmed
  and finely sliced
4 mushrooms, diced
4 free-range eggs
2 tbsp milk of choice
Freshly ground black
  pepper (optional)
25g Cheddar, grated
  (optional)

STORAGE

Can be stored in a sealed container in the fridge for up to 2 days or frozen for up to 1 month. Wrap individual rosti in parchment paper. Defrost at room temperature and reheat before serving.

DAIRY-FREE

Use a hard vegan cheese and olive oil instead of Cheddar and butter.

Preheat the oven to 180°C/160°C fan/gas mark 4 and grease six holes of a muffin tin.

Melt half the butter in a small saucepan over a medium heat. Squeeze out the excess liquid from the potato, then add to the pan and stir to coat it well. Divide between the muffin holes, pressing down firmly with the back of a spoon. Place in the oven and roast for 15 minutes, or until soft.

Meanwhile, using the same saucepan, melt the remaining butter and add the pepper, leek and mushrooms. Cover with a lid and cook for 3 minutes, or until soft, stirring occasionally.

Whisk the eggs and milk together in a small jug and season with black pepper, if using.

Remove the rosti from the oven and divide the vegetables between them. Pour in the egg mixture, sprinkle with the grated cheese, if using, and bake in the oven for 10–12 minutes, until the tops are firm to the touch.

Leave them to cool for 1 minute, before loosening from the muffin holes and sliding on to a plate. Serve warm or cold.

TIP You can adapt this recipe by adding ham, asparagus tips, red onion, broccoli, or any leftover cooked veg you have in the fridge.

PEANUT BUTTER DIPPING SAUCE

A delish plant-based sauce that you can make in a jiffy and serve with
a tofu dish, such as Crispy Coconut Tofu Stars (see page 161).

SERVES 2–3 CHILDREN

2 tbsp peanut butter
2 tbsp hot water
Juice of ½ lime

Simply combine all the ingredients in a small bowl.

STORAGE

Can be stored in the
fridge in a sealed
container for 3–4 days.
Not suitable for freezing.

NUT-FREE
Use light tahini
paste instead of
peanut butter.

6 MONTHS PLUS

CRISPY COCONUT TOFU STARS

Tofu is a good source of protein and contains nutrients such as calcium, selenium and iron, which are important for growing kids. These nuggets are very soft, so perfect for teething babies over 12 months, and toddlers will love the star shapes. Serve with Peanut Butter Dipping Sauce (see page 159) or Tomato Relish (see page 134).

SERVES 1–2 CHILDREN

120g firm tofu
4 tbsp tamari or light
  soya sauce
1 tbsp runny honey
  or maple syrup
1 tsp mixed dried
  Mediterranean herbs
4 tbsp spelt flour
  or cornflour
1 free-range egg
4 tbsp puffed brown
  rice cereal, crushed,
  or Panko breadcrumbs
2 tbsp desiccated coconut
2 tbsp ground almonds
1 tsp paprika
Drizzle of olive oil

STORAGE

Can be stored in a
sealed container in the
fridge for 2 days. Not
suitable for freezing.

Preheat the oven to 180°C/160°C fan/gas mark 4 and line a baking tray with parchment paper.

To prevent the tofu from going soggy, drain off any excess water by slicing the block horizontally into 3 even slabs and placing a sheet of kitchen paper between each slab and on top. Cover with a weight or press down with your hands. Pat the tofu dry, then use a cookie cutter to cut into star shapes, or use a knife and cut into small cubes.

Place the tamari or soya, honey or maple syrup and herbs in a shallow bowl and mix well to combine. Add the tofu and stir gently to coat in the marinade. Leave for at least 15 minutes, the longer the better. Turn the pieces every now and then.

Set out three bowls – place the flour in the first one, the beaten egg in the second, and combine the crushed rice cereal or Panko breadcrumbs with the desiccated coconut, ground almonds and paprika in the third. Dip the tofu stars first into the flour, then the egg, and finally in the cereal mixture.

Transfer to the prepared baking tray and drizzle with a little olive oil. Bake in the oven for 15–17 minutes, turning them halfway through, until golden and crispy.

GLUTEN-FREE
Use gluten-free
soya sauce or tamari,
gluten-free brown
rice cereal, and
gluten-free flour.

NUT-FREE
Replace almonds
with 2 tbsp more
desiccated coconut.

SOYA-FREE
Swap soya sauce for
coconut amino.

EGG-FREE
Omit egg and add
6–7 tbsp coconut
milk to the flour.

BUTTERNUT SQUASH & KALE MAC 'N' CHEESE

This supercharged mac 'n' cheese is an excellent way to get your kids to eat their veg.

MAKES 5 RAMEKINS

½ butternut squash, peeled and cut into 2cm chunks
2 tbsp olive oil
100g macaroni
20g unsalted butter
20g spelt flour
300ml/1¼ cups milk of choice
60g Parmesan, finely grated
¼ tsp freshly grated nutmeg
Handful of kale, finely chopped
Freshly ground black pepper (optional)
Pinch of fine sea salt
Handful of sage leaves
1 slice of wholemeal bread, toasted, crusts removed, and blitzed into breadcrumbs in a food processor
2 tbsp pumpkin seeds

STORAGE

Can be stored in a sealed container in the fridge for 3 days, or in the freezer for up to 3 months.

Preheat the oven to 220°C/200°C fan/gas mark 7 and line a large roasting tray with baking parchment.

Place the squash on the prepared tray and toss in 1 tablespoon of the oil. Roast for 25 minutes, or until tender and browned at the edges. Remove from the oven and leave to cool slightly.

Meanwhile, bring a large pan of water to the boil and cook the macaroni until almost al dente (2–3 minutes less than the time suggested on the packet). Drain and set aside.

Pop three-quarters of the roasted squash into a food processor and blitz to a purée. Set the rest aside.

To make the sauce, melt the butter in a large saucepan over a medium heat. Add the flour and cook, stirring, for 1 minute. Whisk in the milk and continue to cook, still whisking, until the sauce thickens slightly. Lower the heat and stir in the Parmesan and nutmeg, followed by the squash purée and kale. Remove from the heat and season to taste, if using.

Preheat the grill to high.

Add the macaroni to the sauce and stir well. Divide the pasta mixture between 5 ramekins. Top with the remaining roasted squash, the sage and breadcrumbs. Drizzle with a little olive oil and grill for 8–10 minutes, until golden brown.

Remove from the grill, scatter over the pumpkin seeds and grill for a final few minutes. Serve at once.

DAIRY-FREE
Swap butter for dairy-free spread and use hard Parmesan-style vegan cheese.

GLUTEN-FREE
Use gluten-free macaroni, flour and bread.

BEAN BURRITOS IN BAKED WRAP CUPS

Kidney beans are high in fibre, protein and complex carbohydrates, which help stabilise blood sugar levels. They provide a complete protein when combined with rice or a grain. These burritos are packed full of veggies, too. Toddlers will enjoy building their own muffin cups – it's messy but lots of fun! Alternatively, serve with rice and your choice of toppings.

SERVES 6 CHILDREN

3 tortilla wraps
1 tbsp olive oil, plus
    extra for greasing
1 small red onion, diced
½ garlic clove, crushed
1 courgette, chopped
    into small cubes
2 small peppers (1 red
    and 1 yellow), deseeded
    and roughly chopped
½ small butternut squash,
    peeled and chopped
1 × 400g tin kidney beans,
    rinsed and drained
1 × 400g tin cherry or
    chopped tomatoes
1 tsp smoked paprika
½ tsp dried oregano
100g cooked brown rice
Guacamole (see page 50)
1–2 tsp sour cream
30g Cheddar, grated

Preheat the oven to 180°C/160°C fan /gas mark 4 and lightly grease six holes of a muffin tin.

Use a 10cm cookie cutter to cut two rounds from each tortilla. Place the tortilla circles in the holes and use the bottom of a glass to push them in. Brush with a little olive oil and cook in the oven for 4–5 minutes, or until slightly golden. Remove and leave to cool.

Place the 1 tablespoon oil in a saucepan over a medium heat. Add the onion and fry for 3–5 minutes, or until soft. Add the garlic and cook for a further minute.

Stir in the courgette, peppers, squash, kidney beans, tomatoes, paprika and oregano, and bring to the boil. Cover with a tightly fitting lid, reduce the heat and simmer for 20 minutes, or until the squash is tender. Remove the lid for the last 5 minutes and increase the heat to reduce the sauce.

Using a potato masher, mash the bean mixture to your desired consistency, or blitz with a hand blender to a mush.

Fill each cup with some brown rice, burrito mixture, guacamole, sour cream and Cheddar to serve.

12 MONTHS PLUS

GLUTEN-FREE
Use gluten-free tortillas or wraps.

DAIRY-FREE
Use oat crème fraîche and a hard vegan cheese.

SWEET POTATO & ROSEMARY WAFFLES

These crunchy waffles are far more nutritious and flavoursome than shop-bought ones. Serve with Crunchy Chicken Dippers (see page 124), Avocado Mayo (see page 133) and Tomato Relish (see page 134).

MAKES 7 WAFFLES

180g/1¾ cups
   porridge oats
40g/¼ cup
   buckwheat flour
3 tsp baking powder
2 free-range eggs
400ml/1¾ cups milk
   of choice
4 tbsp unsalted
   butter, melted
1 garlic clove, crushed
½ medium sweet potato,
   peeled and finely grated
Sprig of rosemary,
   leaves finely chopped,
   or 2 tsp dried

Blitz the oats in a food processor with a grinding blade until you have a flour-like consistency.

Tip into a bowl and combine with the rest of the ingredients, taking care not to over-stir.

Turn your waffle maker to the highest setting and pour a ladleful of the mixture into the lower plate. Be careful not to overfill it or the mixture will come pouring out of the sides. Close the lid and let the waffle cook for 5 minutes. Repeat until you have used up all the batter.

GLUTEN-FREE
Use gluten-free oats.

DAIRY-FREE
Use dairy-free spread or olive oil.

STORAGE

Can be stored in a sealed container in the fridge for 3 days, or in the freezer for up to 3 months. Toast in the toaster straight from the freezer.

6
MONTHS
PLUS

CHEESY SWEETCORN & COURGETTE PATTIES

Courgettes are not usually a toddler's number one veggie. It's probably because they often have a soggy texture, but these crispy patties will be a winner. The chickpea (gram) flour absorbs the moisture and is a great source of protein – learn how to make your own on page 87. Serve with some zesty hummus (see pages 47–48) or guacamole (see page 50).

MAKES 8 PATTIES

100g/¾ cup frozen
  sweetcorn
½ medium courgette,
  grated
½ apple, grated
  (and peeled for babies
  under 12 months old)
½ small onion, grated
½ red pepper, deseeded
  and finely chopped
5 tbsp chickpea (gram)
  flour (or spelt flour)
1 free-range egg
20g Cheddar, grated
1 tbsp olive or coconut oil

Place the sweetcorn in a small bowl and pour some boiling water over to defrost it. Drain and set aside.

Squeeze out any excess juice from the courgette and apple. This is key, otherwise the patties will be soggy.

In a bowl, combine the corn, courgette, apple, onion, red pepper, chickpea flour, egg and cheese, and mix well.

Using your hands, shape the mixture into small patties. Place them on a plate, cover and chill in the fridge for at least 10 minutes to firm up.

Place the oil in a frying pan over a medium heat. Add the patties and fry for 4 minutes on each side.

STORAGE

Can be stored in a sealed container in the fridge for 2 days. Not suitable for freezing.

DAIRY-FREE
Use a hard
vegan cheese.

6 MONTHS PLUS

ROASTED CHICKPEA BITES TWO WAYS – ITALIAN PIZZA OR SWEET & SPICY

Crunchy little snacks you can take with you when you are out and about. Super-easy to make with two yummy flavours to try.

SERVES 4 CHILDREN

1 × 400g tin chickpeas, rinsed and drained
2 tbsp olive oil

Italian Pizza
2 tsp mixed dried Mediterranean herbs
2 tsp smoked paprika
Pinch of fine sea salt

Sweet & Spicy
2 tsp ground allspice
2 tsp coconut sugar or light muscovado sugar

STORAGE

Once cooled, can be stored in a glass jar for 3 days. Not suitable for freezing.

12 MONTHS PLUS

Preheat the oven to 200°C/180°C fan/gas mark 5.

Spread the chickpeas on kitchen paper and gently pat dry. It's important that they are totally dry before you toss them with the olive oil, as damp chickpeas won't crisp up in the oven.

Spread them out on a baking tray, drizzle the olive oil over the top and shake to coat. Roast for 30–40 minutes, or until brown and crunchy. Check frequently towards the end of the cooking time to avoid burning.

Transfer to a bowl and sprinkle over the Italian Pizza or Sweet & Spicy flavourings.

Eat warm or at room temperature.

CARROT & CHEDDAR QUINOA BITES

A mess-free vegetarian dish that is packed with protein and fibre.
Parsley is a good source of antioxidants and vitamin C, too.
These are yummy hot or cold.

MAKES 16 BITES

60g/⅓ cup quinoa (180g/
1 cup cooked weight)
180ml/¾ cup water or
vegetable or chicken
stock (homemade
or very low salt)
1 firm pear, cored and
grated (and peeled
if your baby is under
12 months old)
1 large carrot, peeled
and finely grated
95g Cheddar, finely grated
1 tbsp finely chopped
fresh parsley
1 free-range egg, beaten

STORAGE

Can be stored in a sealed
container in the fridge for
3 days, or in the freezer
for up to 2 months. Defrost
at room temperature and
reheat to serve.

Preheat the oven to 180°C/160°C fan/gas mark 4 and line
a baking tray with parchment paper.

If you are using uncooked quinoa, rinse it and place in a pan
with the water or stock. Cover with a lid and bring to the boil.
Reduce the heat and simmer for 15 minutes, or until the liquid
is absorbed and the quinoa is cooked. Remove from the heat
and leave the lid on for 5 minutes to allow it to fluff up.
Then remove the lid and leave to cool.

Squeeze out any excess juice from the grated pear and
carrot and place them in a medium bowl. Add the quinoa,
cheese, parsley and beaten egg, and mix well to combine.

Using your hands, shape the mixture into small balls
and transfer to the prepared baking tray. Bake for 20–22
minutes, or until golden and firm to the touch, turning
them halfway through.

Remove from the oven and transfer to a wire rack to cool.

DAIRY-FREE
Use a hard
vegan cheese.

EGG-FREE
Swap egg for
1 heaped tsp chickpea
(gram) flour and
3 tsp water.

CHEESY BUTTERBEAN BITES

These scrumptious bites are perfect for a first baby-led weaning food.
The texture is really soft so they melt in the mouth.

MAKES 18 BITES

½ apple, grated
(peeled for children
under 12 months)
1 × 400g tin butterbeans,
rinsed, drained and
patted dry
75g Emmenthal or
Cheddar, grated
1 spring onion, chopped
2 tsp chopped chives
1 tsp grainy mustard
(optional)
Splash of olive oil
or milk, to glaze

Preheat the oven to 180°C/160°C fan/gas mark 4 and line
a baking tray with parchment paper.

Squeeze out the excess liquid from the apple, then place in
a food processor with the butterbeans, cheese, spring onion,
chives and mustard, if using. Blitz to a paste.

Using your hands, shape the mixture into small walnut-sized
balls and place on the prepared baking tray. Use a folk to
flatten them slightly. Brush with olive oil or milk and bake for
20–25 minutes, or until golden and firm to the touch, turning
halfway through. (The time will vary depending on the size
of your bites, so check after 15 minutes.)

STORAGE

Can be stored in a sealed
container in the fridge for
3 days, or in the freezer
for up to 3 months. Defrost
at room temperature and
reheat in the oven to serve.

DAIRY-FREE
Use a hard
vegan cheese.

6
MONTHS
PLUS

CHAPTER FIVE

BABY-LED & FAMILY SWEET TREATS

Crumbles, doughnuts, cookies, lollies and ice cream –
all your favourite treats packed with nutrition and yet
not a grain of refined white sugar in sight. Enjoy!

CHAMOMILE & VANILLA TEETHING BISCUITS

Both chamomile and ginger have anti-inflammatory properties that will help soothe painful gums during teething. This biscuit has a crusty edge and soft centre, so is perfect for little ones to chomp on.

MAKES 13-14 BISCUITS

1 large sweet potato, peeled and cut into chunks
2 chamomile tea bags
1 tbsp ground flax seeds
2 tbsp milk of choice
½ tsp vanilla extract
1 banana
1 small carrot, peeled and finely grated
90g/¾ cup fine porridge oats
30g/2 tbsp spelt or wholemeal flour
1 tsp grated fresh root ginger
1 tbsp coconut oil, melted

STORAGE

Can be stored in an airtight container for 3–4 days, or in the freezer for up to 1 month. If they go a bit soft, pop them in the oven to crisp up.

Preheat the oven to 180°C/160°C fan/gas mark 4 and line a baking tray with parchment paper.

Place the sweet potato and tea bags in a saucepan half-filled with cold water. Cover and bring to the boil. Reduce the heat and simmer for 6–7 minutes, or until the sweet potato is soft.

Drain the water and discard the tea bags. Return the sweet potato to the pan and place on the heat for 30 seconds to dry out – you don't want it to be too wet.

Mix the ground flax seeds and milk together in a small bowl.

Tip the sweet potato into a separate bowl, add the vanilla and mash them together. Leave to cool, then add the banana and mash again until smooth. Stir in the flax seeds and milk, carrot, oats, flour, ginger and coconut oil, and mix together.

Wet your hands and roll the mixture into 13–14 balls, then place them on the prepared baking tray and flatten slightly. Bake for 18–20 minutes, or until golden.

Remove from the oven and leave to firm up on the tray for a few minutes, then transfer the biscuits to a wire rack to cool.

6 MONTHS PLUS

GLUTEN-FREE
Use rice flour instead of spelt.

SPICED CRACKERS WITH AN ORANGE TWIST

These protein-rich spiced crackers are great paired with my Zingy Hummus Trio (see page 47). A perfect snack to keep hunger at bay!

MAKES 25–30 CRACKERS

90g/¾ cup fine porridge oats, plus extra for dusting
1 × 400g tin chickpeas, rinsed and drained
3–4 tbsp olive or sesame oil
2 tsp ground cinnamon
1 tsp freshly grated root ginger
Zest of 1 orange and 3 tbsp orange juice
Pinch of fine sea salt (not for children under 12 months)

STORAGE

Can be stored in a sealed container for 3–4 days, or in the freezer for up to 1 month. If they go a bit soft, pop them in the oven to crisp up.

GLUTEN-FREE
Use gluten-free oats.

Preheat the oven to 180°C/160°C fan/gas mark 4.

Blitz the oats in a food processor with a grinding blade until you have a flour-like consistency. Remove 2 tablespoons of the oat flour and set aside.

Add the chickpeas to the processor and blitz again.

While the machine is running, add 2 tablespoons of the oil, followed by the cinnamon, ginger, orange zest and juice. Add more olive oil, a tablespoon at a time, while the machine is running, until the mixture comes together in a ball. If it's too sticky, add some of the reserved ground oats.

Line a baking tray with parchment paper and dust with the last of the reserved oat flour. Place the dough on top, then lay another sheet of parchment paper over the top. Gently flatten it with your hands, then roll it out until it is around 5mm thick. Do not pick up the dough or move it, or it might break.

Remove the top layer of parchment paper and use a knife to lightly score the dough into crackers. Prick each cracker with a fork a couple of times – this will prevent them from rising and they will bake more evenly. Bake for 30–35 minutes, or until golden and firm to the touch.

Leave to cool completely on the tray before breaking into crackers.

APPLE OATCAKES

The cutest little oatcakes to take on family adventures!
Soft enough for babies with painful gums.

MAKES 18–20 OATCAKES

125g/1¼ cups fine
   porridge oats
30g/¼ cup
   sunflower seeds
20g/1 heaped tbsp
   coconut sugar or light
   muscovado sugar
20ml maple, date
   or rice syrup
35g unsalted butter
½ apple, peeled and
   finely grated
1 tsp ground cinnamon

STORAGE

Can be stored in an
airtight container for
3–4 days, or in the freezer
for up to 3 months.

6 MONTHS PLUS

Preheat the oven to 180°C/160°C fan/gas mark 4 and line
a baking tray with parchment paper.

Blitz the oats and sunflower seeds in a food processor with
a grinding blade until you have a flour-like consistency.

Meanwhile, melt the sugar, syrup and butter together in
a small saucepan over a low heat.

Place the apple, cinnamon and ground oats and seeds in a
bowl and stir in the sugar mixture. Combine the ingredients
to form a ball.

Place the dough between two pieces of parchment paper
and roll out to 2–3mm thick. Use a cookie cutter to cut into
little shapes.

Transfer them to the prepared baking tray and bake for
11–12 minutes, or until golden and firm to the touch.

Remove from the oven and leave to firm up on the tray for a
few minutes, then transfer the oatcakes to a wire rack to cool.

GLUTEN-FREE
Use gluten-free oats.

BRAIN BOX COOKIES

Saffron is a spice that helps to modulate the stress response and can also improve focus and concentration. It pairs beautifully with orange to make these scrumptious cookies. The sunflower seeds provide a boost of choline, an important brain food for learning.

MAKES 18-20 COOKIES

350g/2¼ cups spelt or wholemeal flour
60g/¼ cup coconut sugar or light muscovado sugar
½ tsp bicarbonate of soda
10g/2 tsp sunflower seeds
Pinch of fine sea salt (not for children under 12 months)
Zest of 1 large orange
125g unsalted butter
60g/¼ cup maple syrup or honey (not for children under 12 months)
1 free-range egg, beaten
1 saffron strand, soaked in some warm water for 5-10 minutes

Preheat the oven to 180°C/160°C fan/gas mark 4 and line a baking tray with parchment paper.

Mix the dry ingredients with the orange zest in a large bowl.

Melt the butter with the maple syrup or honey in a saucepan over a low heat.

Stir the butter mixture into the dry ingredients. Remove the saffron strand from the water and add to the bowl, along with the egg, and mix everything together well.

Using your hands, shape the dough into 18–20 walnut-sized pieces. Transfer them to the prepared baking tray, placing them 1.5–2cm apart. Flatten each ball slightly with a fork, so they are about 5mm thick. Bake for 13–15 minutes, or until golden brown.

Remove from the oven and leave to firm up on the tray for a few minutes, then transfer the cookies to a wire rack to cool.

STORAGE

Can be stored in an airtight container for 3–4 days, or in the freezer for up to 1 month. If they go a bit soft, pop them in the oven to crisp up.

6 MONTHS PLUS

DAIRY-FREE
Replace the butter with dairy-free spread.

GLUTEN-FREE
Use 300g gluten-free flour plus 50g ground almonds.

EGG-FREE
Swap egg for 1 tbsp ground flax seeds combined with 2½ tbsp water.

APPLE & RASPBERRY CRUMBLE BITES

6 MONTHS PLUS

Crumble is a big thing in our family. However, when it came to weaning, it wasn't the easiest food for our team of little people to tackle. So, I came up with these crumble bites and we've never looked back. They've become our go-to Sunday lunch pudding served with Bay Custard (see page 193). A great little pick-me-up after a chilly walk.

MAKES 16–25 MINI SQUARES

120g unsalted butter or coconut oil
1 large banana, mashed
3 tbsp maple syrup
125g/¾ cup spelt or wholemeal flour
125g/1¼ cups porridge oats
1 tsp baking powder
2 tsp ground cinnamon
1 tsp ground mixed spice
¼ tsp fine sea salt (not for children under 12 months)
1 free-range egg
2 medium apples, peeled, cored and cut into 1cm cubes
125g fresh or frozen raspberries (if using frozen, defrost and drain off any liquid)

Preheat the oven to 180°C/160°C fan/gas mark 4 and line a 22cm square baking tin with parchment paper.

Melt the butter or oil in a small saucepan over a medium heat, then remove from the heat. Add the mashed banana to the pan and stir in the maple syrup.

In a large mixing bowl, combine the flour, oats, baking powder, cinnamon, mixed spice and salt, if using, then stir in the banana mixture and the egg. It will form a wet crumble. Gently fold in the apple and raspberries.

Spoon the mixture into the prepared tin, making sure it is evenly spread. Bake for 30–33 minutes, or until slightly golden.

Remove from the oven and leave to cool for 20 minutes before taking out of the tin in one piece. Crumble is its name, so be gentle! Wait until it's completely cool before slicing into squares.

STORAGE

Can be stored in an airtight container for 3–4 days, or in the freezer for up to 3 months.

GLUTEN-FREE
Use gluten-free flour, baking powder and oats.

EGG-FREE
Replace egg with 4 tbsp ground flax seeds combined with 5 tbsp water. You'll need to cut it into squares before cooking.

STRAWBERRY & BUCKWHEAT MINI DOUGHNUTS

Everyone loves a doughnut, and these are packed with nutrients without a grain of refined sugar in sight. The date syrup gives them a deep caramel flavour, while the strawberries make them moist and succulent. The doughnut shape is easy for little fingers to pick up, but if you don't have a doughnut tin, make mini muffins instead – you'll just need to cook them for 2–3 minutes longer.

MAKES 12 MINI DOUGHNUTS

60ml/¼ cup milk
   of choice
1 tsp white wine or
   apple cider vinegar
1 tsp vanilla extract
2 tbsp date syrup
2 tbsp light olive oil,
   plus extra for greasing
160g/1 cup spelt flour
40g/¼ cup
   buckwheat flour
1 tsp baking powder
¼ tsp fine sea salt
   (not for children
   under 12 months)
1 tsp ground cinnamon
3 strawberries, hulled
   and diced

Preheat the oven to 180°C/160°C fan/gas mark 4 and grease a mini doughnut or mini muffin tin.

Whisk the milk, vinegar, vanilla extract, date syrup and oil in a jug and set aside.

Mix all the remaining ingredients except the strawberries in a bowl, then pour in the contents of the jug. Stir until just mixed, then gently fold in the strawberries.

Pour the mixture into the prepared tin and bake for 12–14 minutes, or until the doughnuts have risen and the batter is no longer wet.

Remove from the oven and leave for 5 minutes before removing from the tin.

STORAGE

Can be stored in an airtight container for 3–4 days, or in the freezer for up to 3 months.

GLUTEN-FREE
Use gluten-free flour.

6 MONTHS PLUS

MINI AVOCADO, CARROT & BLUEBERRY MUFFINS

Big muffins are rather overwhelming and wasteful when weaning.
This is why I've created a mini version, which is also naturally gluten-free. Avocado is rich in healthy fats and high in potassium, a mineral that has an important role in growth and muscle-building. These scrumptious little morsels don't last a second in our house!

MAKES 20–22 MINI MUFFINS

2 tbsp sunflower seeds
200g/2 cups ground almonds
1 tsp ground ginger
½ tsp baking powder
¼ tsp fine sea salt (not for children under 12 months)
½ avocado, peeled and stoned
1 banana
1 small carrot, peeled and finely grated
Zest of 1 orange
2 tbsp honey (not for children under 12 months) or maple syrup
1 free-range egg
50g/¼ cup blueberries, halved

Preheat the oven to 180°C/160°C fan/gas mark 4.
You will need a silicone mini muffin tin.

Blitz the sunflower seeds in a food processor until they resemble breadcrumbs. Transfer them to a medium bowl, add the ground almonds, ginger, baking powder and salt, if using, and stir to combine.

Place the avocado, banana, carrot, orange zest, honey or maple syrup and egg in another bowl and blitz using a hand blender. For fussy eaters, make sure the carrot is well blended.

Fold in the almond mixture, followed by the blueberries.

Divide the mixture equally between the holes of the mini muffin tin and bake for 13–15 minutes, or until firm to the touch and lightly golden.

Remove from the oven and leave to cool slightly in the tin before transferring to a wire rack.

STORAGE

Can be stored in an airtight container for 3 days, or in the freezer for up to 2 months.

GLUTEN-FREE
Use gluten-free baking powder.

EGG-FREE
Replace the egg with 1 tbsp flax seeds combined with 2½ tbsp water.

NUT-FREE
Use 200g sunflower seeds instead of ground almonds, and replace the ground sunflower seeds with 2 tbsp ground flax seeds.

STRAWBERRY PILLOWS

A real treat to bake at the weekends when you have a bit of time and a little
helper at your side. The pastry is quick and easy to make and the homemade
strawberry and vanilla filling is so much healthier than shop-bought jam.

MAKES 8 LARGE OR 16 SMALL PILLOWS

250g/1½ cups spelt flour,
plus extra for dusting
150g unsalted butter,
grated straight from
the fridge
3 tbsp honey or rice syrup
Zest of 1 lemon
50ml ice-cold water
8 tsp Strawberry & Vanilla
Chia Jam (see page 192)
1 free-range egg, lightly
whisked with a fork,
to seal and glaze

STORAGE

Can be stored in an
airtight container
for 3 days, or in the
freezer for up to 2
months. Defrost at
room temperature.

12 MONTHS PLUS

Preheat the oven to 180°C/160°C fan/gas mark 4.

Place the flour and butter in a bowl and rub together until
they resemble breadcrumbs. Stir in the honey or syrup and
the lemon zest, then slowly add the ice-cold water and mix
with a knife until the pastry starts to bind.

Turn out on to a lightly floured surface and gently work until
you have a smooth dough. Try not to overwork it – visible
spots of butter are fine. Wrap the pastry in a beeswax wrap
or clingfilm and chill in the fridge for 30 minutes.

On a lightly floured surface, roll out the pastry to a thickness
of 2–3mm. Cut into 16 large or 32 small squares. Transfer half
the squares to the prepared tray and blind-bake in the oven
for 10 minutes. These will be the bottoms of the pillows.

Remove them from the oven and dollop ½–1 teaspoon jam
on each square, then brush the edges of the pastry with a little
egg. Place a second layer of pastry on top of each one, sealing
the edges with a fork. Prick the tops with a fork, then glaze
with the remaining egg. Bake in the oven for 20 minutes,
or until the pastry is evenly browned.

Remove from the oven and leave to cool on the tray for
a few minutes, before transferring to a wire rack.

GLUTEN-FREE
Use gluten-free flour
and baking powder.

DAIRY-FREE
Use dairy-free spread
instead of butter.

EGG-FREE
Use milk instead
of egg.

BRAINY BLISS BALLS

Carrot cake is a family favourite, so I wanted my team of toddlers to experience its wonderful flavours. You can use any nuts or seeds – I have chosen walnuts as they contain high amounts of omega 3, an essential fatty acid that feeds the brain. These no-bake balls make a splendid birthday cake, too. Flatten one side of each ball so it sits flat on the surface and place a candle on top. It's a win-win situation: the birthday boy/girl gets lots of candles to blow out and everyone else gets their own carrot ball to eat.

MAKES 20-22 BALLS

55g dried apricots
(ideally unsulphured)
5 Medjool dates
85g/¾ cup porridge oats
85g walnuts or
pumpkin seeds
85g/¾ cup desiccated
coconut
1 tsp ground cinnamon
2 tsp ground mixed spice
1 large carrot, peeled and
finely grated
1 tbsp coconut oil, melted
Juice of 1 tangerine
5 tbsp hulled hemp
seeds, or extra
desiccated coconut

STORAGE

Can be stored in an airtight container for 5 days, or in the freezer for up to 2 months. They taste just as good when slightly frozen.

Place the apricots and dates in a small bowl. Pour boiling water over the top and soak for 5 minutes, then drain and finely chop.

Place the oats, walnuts or pumpkin seeds, coconut, cinnamon and mixed spice in a food processor and blitz until they resemble fine breadcrumbs. Transfer to a medium bowl.

Squeeze out any excess liquid from the grated carrot and set aside. Place the drained carrots, dates and apricots in the food processor and pulse until everything is broken down. While the machine is still running, add the coconut oil, then the carrot and tangerine juice. You might need to use a spatula to scrape down the sides.

Tip the carrot mixture into the bowl with the oat mixture and mix together well.

Using your hands, shape the mixture into 20–22 small balls, then roll them in the hemp seeds or more desiccated coconut.

GLUTEN-FREE
Use gluten-free oats.

BEETS TO THE RESCUE BLISS BALLS

My little nieces adore these rosy-coloured treats, even though they would
normally turn their noses up at beetroot. Beetroot really helps little people
who struggle with constipation, as it contains insoluble fibre – the type
that is not absorbed by the body but helps move food through the gut.
Don't be alarmed if their stools are slightly red for a day!

MAKES 12–14 BALLS

85g/⅔ cup sunflower
seeds
1 large beetroot, cooked
without vinegar
1 medium banana
85g/¾ cup porridge oats
1 tbsp ground chia seeds
1 tsp ground cinnamon
1 tbsp maple syrup
(optional)
1 tbsp coconut oil, melted
5 tbsp hulled hemp
seeds, extra chia
seeds or desiccated
coconut (optional)

Place the sunflower seeds in a food processor and blitz
until they resemble breadcrumbs. Transfer to a small bowl.

Place the beetroot in the food processor and blend to a purée.
Add the banana, oats, chia seeds, cinnamon, maple syrup,
if using, coconut oil and blitzed sunflower seeds, and pulse
until you have a smooth paste.

If you have a toddler, you might like to get them involved at
this point – it's nice and messy! Using your hands, shape the
mixture into walnut-sized balls, then roll them in the hemp
seeds, chia seeds or desiccated coconut, or a mixture,
ensuring they get an even coating.

STORAGE

Can be stored in a sealed
container in the fridge
for 3–4 days, or in the
freezer for up to 1 month.
They taste good even
when still slightly frozen.

GLUTEN-FREE
Use gluten-free oats.

6
MONTHS
PLUS

NUTTY SWEET POTATO TOASTS

These make a delicious alternative to toasted bread. There are so many different sweet and savoury toppings you could try – I've included my favourite here but they also go well with Pumpkin Seed Pesto (see page 121) or Minty Pea & Ricotta Dip (see page 49).

MAKES 4-5 SLICES

1 large sweet
   potato, peeled
2 tbsp almond, peanut
   or cashew butter
2 tbsp Mango Chia jam
   (see page 192)

STORAGE

Can be stored in a
sealed container in
the fridge for 2 days.
They do not freeze well.

Cut the sweet potato lengthways into thin slices about 3mm thick.

Pop them in the toaster for 5 minutes, then toast them again, until they are cooked through.

Slather on some nut butter, then top with some jam.

NUT-FREE
Use tahini paste
or sunflower
seed butter.

TRIO OF CHIA JAMS

A simple way to make 'jam' without using refined sugar.
Serve as a compote with Greek-style yoghurt, granola,
porridge, rice pudding, waffles or pancakes.

EACH RECIPE MAKES ½ JAM JAR (100ML)

MANGO CHIA JAM

1 mango, peeled and stoned
1 tsp chia seeds

Blitz the mango with the chia seeds in
a food processor for 1 minute. Leave for
5 minutes then blend again for 30 seconds.

Pour the jam into a warm glass jar and
leave to thicken for up to 10 minutes.

BLACKBERRY & APPLE CHIA JAM

1 large apple, peeled, cored and sliced
  (Gala or Pink Lady)
25g frozen blackberries
1 tsp chia seeds

Place a saucepan over a low heat. Add
all the ingredients and cook gently for
5 minutes, or until the apple is soft and
the berries have broken down into a pulp.

Pour the jam into a warm glass jar and
leave to thicken for up to 10 minutes.

STRAWBERRY & VANILLA CHIA JAM

90g/1½ cups strawberries, hulled
1 tsp maple syrup
½ tsp vanilla extract
1 tsp chia seeds

Place a saucepan over a low heat. Add all
the ingredients and cook gently for 5 minutes,
or until the strawberries have broken down
into a pulp and the jam has start to thicken.

Pour the jam into a warm glass jar and
leave to thicken for up to 10 minutes.

STORAGE

The Mango Chia Jam can be
stored in the fridge for 4 days.
Not suitable for freezing.

The Blackberry & Apple and
Strawberry & Vanilla Chia
Jams can be stored in the
fridge for 10 days, or in the
freezer for up to 3 months.

BAY CUSTARD

A thick eggy custard that is delicious served warm with Blackberry & Apple Crumble (see page 195) or cold with fresh fruit, such as juicy, sliced peaches.

(see page 195)

MAKES MEDIUM JUG (300ML)

1 heaped tsp cornflour
240ml/1 cup milk
    of choice
2 bay leaves
2 egg yolks
½ tsp vanilla extract
1 tsp honey or maple syrup

STORAGE

Can be stored in the fridge for 3 days. Not suitable for freezing.

12 MONTHS PLUS

Place the cornflour and a little of the milk in a small saucepan and mix to a paste. Slowly add the remaining milk, stirring all the time.

Add the bay leaves to the pan and place over a low heat to warm through.

Meanwhile, beat the egg yolks, vanilla and honey or maple syrup together in a small bowl until pale and creamy.

Discard the bay leaves, then slowly pour the egg mixture into the milk, whisking well. Continue to heat for a few minutes until the custard starts to thicken.

EGG-FREE
Omit the eggs and cook for a little longer.

BLACKBERRY & APPLE CRUMBLE

A wonderful autumn recipe made from hedgerow fruits, perfect as
a pudding for Sunday lunch or as a teatime treat. Serve with vanilla
ice cream or Bay Custard (see page 193).

MAKES 1 LARGE OR 5 MINI CRUMBLES

2 apples, peeled,
   cored and chopped
200g blackberries
Zest and juice of 1 orange
100g/1 cup fine
   porridge oats
25g/¼ cup ground
   almonds
25g coconut sugar or
   light muscovado sugar
50g unsalted butter

STORAGE

Can be stored in
the fridge for 3 days,
or in the freezer for
up to 3 months.

Preheat the oven to 180°C/160°C fan/gas mark 4.

Arrange the apples and blackberries in a medium ovenproof
dish, or divide evenly between 5 large ramekins. Pour the
orange juice over the top of the fruit.

Make the crumble by rubbing the oats, ground almonds, sugar,
butter and orange zest together in a bowl until they resemble
rough breadcrumbs. Scatter evenly over the top of the fruit
in the ovenproof dish, or spoon 2 tablespoons of the topping
into each ramekin.

Bake in the oven for 25–30 minutes, or until slightly brown.

GLUTEN-FREE
Use gluten-free oats.

DAIRY-FREE
Use dairy-free
spread or coconut
oil instead of
butter.

BERRY NICE ICE LOLLIES

RASPBERRY & MANGO

These refreshing ice lollies are
a lovely mixture of tropical fruits
delicately spiced with turmeric.

MAKES 6–8 ICE LOLLIES
125g raspberries
½ pineapple, peeled, cored and chopped
1 mango, peeled and stoned
Juice of 1 orange
½ tsp ground turmeric

Place the raspberries and pineapple
in a food processor and blitz. Pour
into 6–8 ice lolly moulds.

Clean the food processor, then add
the mango, orange juice and turmeric
and blitz. Carefully pour on top of
the raspberry mixture.

Pop an ice lolly stick into each mould
and leave to freeze for at least 3 hours.

STORAGE

Can be stored in the
freezer for up to 3 months.

MARBLED BERRY

Perfect for teething babies, and a lovely
option for older children on hot days
after school or a long summer walk.

MAKES 6–8 ICE LOLLIES
75g frozen mixed berries
240ml/1 cup coconut milk
Small handful of baby spinach
2 tbsp coconut yoghurt
½ tsp vanilla extract

Place the mixed berries, coconut milk
and spinach in a food processor and
blitz to a purée.

Mix the yoghurt and vanilla in a small jug.

Pour a little of the berry mixture into
6–8 ice lolly moulds, then add a heaped
teaspoon of the vanilla yoghurt. Finally
top with some more berry mixture.

Pop an ice lolly stick in each mould and
stir gently to create a marbled effect.
Leave to freeze for at least 3 hours.

FROZEN KEFIR BERRY DROPS

Keep a stash of these fruity buttons in your freezer for when your
baby is teething, or your toddler is hungry for a sweet snack.

1 tsp vanilla extract
1 tbsp honey (not for
   children under 12
   months) or maple syrup
125ml/½ cup kefir
   or Greek-style
   natural yoghurt
50g/¼ cup fresh or frozen
   blueberries, halved
Freeze-dried raspberry
   or strawberry sprinkles
   (available in the baking
   section of larger
   supermarkets)

Stir the vanilla and honey or maple syrup into the kefir.

Line a small baking tray with parchment paper (it will need
to be small enough to fit in your freezer). Drop teaspoonfuls
of the kefir mixture on to the parchment paper, spacing
them 1cm or so apart.

Pop halve blueberries or some freeze-dried berry sprinkles
on to each one.

Place the tray in the freezer for at least 3 hours.

DAIRY-FREE
Use coconut yoghurt
instead of kefir.

STORAGE

Can be stored in
the freezer for up to
3 months. Once the
berry drops are frozen,
you can transfer them
to a plastic bag.

6
MONTHS
PLUS

STRAWBERRY & PEANUT BUTTER NANA NICE-CREAM

This is such a great healthy alternative to ice cream. Kids love it and it's perfect for those who don't eat dairy. Made from three simple ingredients, it's a brilliant way of using up overripe bananas.

SERVES 3-4 CHILDREN

3–4 overripe
    bananas, sliced
250g fresh or frozen
    strawberries, hulled
2 tbsp peanut butter
    (salt-free for children
    under 12 months)

STORAGE

Can be stored
in the freezer for
up to 3 months.

6 MONTHS PLUS

Put the banana slices in a sealed plastic bag in the freezer for at least 2 hours.

Place the frozen bananas in a food processor with the strawberries and peanut butter and blitz. You may need to scrape down the sides of the food processor a couple of times to combine everything well.

Serve immediately or freeze for a further 2–3 hours, if you prefer your Nice-Cream more solid.

NUT-FREE
Replace peanut butter
with Greek-style yoghurt,
kefir, sunflower seed
butter, silken tofu
or tahini.

APPLE DOUGHNUT RINGS

This is the easiest last-minute snack for a hungry toddler, and a great
way of giving them a treat that contains protein and healthy fats.
They will also love to help you make them.

MAKES A SNACK FOR 1 ADULT & 1 TODDLER

1 apple
2 tsp nut butter
   or cream cheese

Topping ideas
Raisins, cranberries,
   ground cinnamon,
   honey, maple syrup,
   squeezy chocolate
   sauce, berries,
   chocolate chips,
   strawberry or raspberry
   freeze-dried sprinkles

Core the apple and slice it horizontally to make 4 rings.

Spread the nut butter or cream cheese on to one side
of each ring.

Let your kids add the toppings – let them experiment
with all sorts of combinations!

NUT-FREE
Use tahini paste
or pumpkin seed
butter.

STORAGE

They do not freeze
or refrigerate well –
eat quickly!

12
MONTHS
PLUS

ELDERFLOWER & BERRY JELLY

This homemade jelly is full of vitamin-rich fresh berries that taste
wonderful with fragrant elderflower.

MAKES 6 JELLIES

5 gelatine leaves or 2
heaped tbsp grass-fed
beef gelatine powder
or 2 heaped tbsp
vegan agar flakes
500ml/2 cups fresh apple
and elderberry juice,
or apple juice with 2 tsp
elderflower cordial
Handful of mixed fresh
berries, sliced

Can be stored in the
fridge for 2–3 days.
Not suitable for freezing.

Place the gelatine leaves in a bowl of cold water.

Pour 300ml of the apple and elderberry juice into a small
saucepan and warm gently over a low heat. (Leave the rest
in the fridge – you want it as cold as possible.) Take the
juice off the heat before it starts to bubble.

Squeeze the water out of the gelatine, then pop it into
the warmed juice and stir until dissolved.

Pour the cold juice into the warm and mix well. Transfer
to a jug and pour into 6 jelly moulds.

Divide the sliced berries between the moulds and transfer
to the fridge to set – this can take anything from 2 to 4 hours.

TIP It can be tricky getting the jellies out of the moulds without
them falling apart. The best way to do this is to place a plate or bowl
over the top and turn it over. If the jellies are being a bit stubborn,
don't shake them. Just turn the moulds over again and dip them
in a bowl of warm water for a few seconds, ensuring the top is
above the water line. This should loosen them.

CHICKEN STOCK

Chicken stock is one the most immune-friendly foods you can give your children. As a traditional cold and cough buster, it works to support our neutrophils, the white blood cells that help us defend against infection. I also give it to my kids when they're off their food or have a sore tummy, as it's so nourishing. As well as being super-healthy, chicken stock enhances the flavours of all types of dishes, so I use it as a base in soups, risotto, lentils and slow-cooked stews. I always prefer it to stock cubes and bouillons, as these do not have the same immune-supporting properties. You can make meat stock from virtually any kind of bones, including chicken, beef, venison, duck, lamb and fish. Most people start with chicken, due to its mild taste. I shared this recipe in *The Good Stuff*, but since it is such an important ingredient to have to hand, here it is again.

MAKES 1–2 LITRES

1 chicken carcass
1 carrot, peeled and
　chopped into 3 pieces
1 celery stick, halved
1 onion, halved, skin on
1 bay leaf
Sprig of parsley
Sprig of thyme
4 peppercorns
1 tbsp apple cider vinegar
　or lemon juice
2 litres/8 cups
　filtered water

Preheat the oven to 180°C/160°C fan/gas mark 4.

Place the carcass in a large flameproof casserole dish and roast in the oven for 20–30 minutes to brown the bones.

Remove the dish from the oven and place it on the hob over a high heat. Add the remaining ingredients and bring the liquid to a boil. Reduce the heat to a slow simmer, or return the dish to the oven at 110°C/90°C fan/gas mark 1–2 for at least 6 hours. Skim off any scum from the top of the stock as it cooks.

Remove from the heat and strain the stock through a sieve, discarding the vegetables and bones. Leave to cool completely.

STORAGE

Can be stored in the fridge for up to 7 days, or in the freezer for up to 3 months. I use soup bags or ice lolly/jelly moulds to freeze individual portions.

CELERY-FREE
Replace with finely chopped fennel or leave out.

VEGETABLE STOCK

Vegetable stock will bring a lovely deep flavour to vegetarian and vegan soups, stews and risottos. You can use a wide range of different vegetables to make the stock and also add in leftover water from veg that you've steamed, as well as any peelings. It's so simple that you will soon get into the habit of making it regularly so that you always have some to hand. Here is a basic recipe to get you started.

MAKES 500ML

1 carrot, peeled and
   roughly chopped
1 small onion,
   cut into wedges
½ leek, cut into rounds
1 celery stick,
   roughly chopped
2 bay leaves
2–3 sprigs of thyme
4 peppercorns
500ml boiling water
1 tsp fine sea salt
   (not for children
   under 12 months)

Place the vegetables, herbs and peppercorns in a 1-litre heatproof glass jar and pour on the boiling water, leaving a gap of 2cm or so at the top for expansion. Pop the lid on and leave to cool.

Transfer to the fridge and let the flavours infuse for at least 12 hours.

Strain the stock through a sieve, discarding the vegetables and herbs. Pour the stock back into the jar, and store in the fridge.

STORAGE

Can be stored in the fridge for 1 week, or in the freezer for up to 3 months. I use soup bags or ice lolly/jelly moulds to freeze individual portions.

CELERY-FREE
Replace with finely chopped fennel or leave out.

SANDWICH FILLINGS

When you are out and about or on a picnic with your little one,
sandwiches are an easy option. Here are some filling suggestions:

Egg and cress mayonnaise
Tuna and sweetcorn with Mediterranean herbs and mayonnaise
Grated carrot, cream cheese and sultanas
Turkey slices, cranberry sauce, lettuce and avocado
Apple, cheese and ham
Raspberries and peanut butter
Strawberries and cream cheese
Cucumber, cream cheese and marmite
Honey and banana with almond butter
Chia jam (see page 192) with cream cheese or nut butter

BAKED POTATO FILLINGS

Jacket potatoes make super-easy and economical lunches and suppers.
I always put a metal skewer through the middle to help them cook
faster and more evenly in the oven. Try these fillings with either white
potatoes or sweet potatoes:

Appley Baked Beans (see page 96) with grated Cheddar
First Guacamole and Mexican Black Bean Pâté (see page 50)
Zingy Hummus Dips (see pages 47–48)
Coconut & Tomato Lentil Curry (see page 113) with Coconut Yoghurt
& Lime Dip (see page 56)
Pumpkin Seed Pesto (see page 121) with diced cooked chicken or turkey
Zesty Lemon & Pesto Dip (see page 56) with flaked mackerel
Lemon & Dill Dip (see page 57) with smoked salmon or flaked cooked
salmon Tahini & Herb Dip (see page 57) with chickpeas
Minty Pea & Ricotta Dip (see page 49)
Trout & Dill Pâté (see page 55)

BABIES UNDER 12 MONTHS

Aim to build in two meals per day by 7 months and 3 meals per day by 10 months.
You can introduce more meals earlier if you prefer.

	MONDAY	TUESDAY	WEDNESDAY
Breakfast	Carrot Cake Porridge	Scrambled Eggs with Red Peppers & Chives	Spiced Orange Quinoa Porridge
Lunch	Mexican Black Bean Pâté	Roasted Carrot & Tangerine Hummus	Lemony Chicken & Orzo Soup
Supper	Carrot & Cheddar Quinoa Bites with steamed veggie batons	Coconut & Tomato Lentil Curry with Yellow Split Pea Flatbread	Salmon & Cod Potato Fish Cakes with Avocado Mayo & broccoli florets

THURSDAY

Cottage Cheese
& Dill Blinis

Celeriac &
Apple Mash

Smokey
Butterbean &
Cashew Casserole
with steamed
veggie batons

FRIDAY

Blackberry & Pear
Millet Porridge

Minty Pea &
Ricotta Dip

Pesto Fish Bites
with Crispy Sweet
Potato Chips

SATURDAY

Cheese & Apple
Eggy Bread

Tuscan Spelt &
Borlotti Bean Soup

Turkey &
Cranberry Sleepy
Casserole with
brown rice

SUNDAY

Raspberry Banana
Pancakes

Root Veggie
Mash

Carrot & Apricot
Falafels with Kefir
Flatbreads and
Tahini & Herb Dip

TODDLERS

These are suitable from 12 months onwards.

	MONDAY	TUESDAY	WEDNESDAY
Breakfast	Nut-free Breakfast Squares with a fruit salad	Lemon & Apricot Granola with Greek-style yoghurt and berries	Appley Baked Beans on toast with Lemon & Blueberry Smoothie Bowl
Mid-morning Snack	Roasted Carrot & Tangerine Hummus with seeded oatcakes	Apple Oatcakes	Sage & Cranberry Chicken Liver Pâté with oatcakes and carrot batons
Lunch	Sweet Potato & Rosemary Waffles with Avocado Mayo & Tomato Relish	Mini Veggie Rosti with Yellow Split Pea Flatbread and cherry tomatoes	Sweetcorn Chickpea Pancakes with cucumber batons and Tahini & Herb Dip
After-nap Snack	Apple & Raspberry Crumble Bites	Chamomile & Vanilla Teething Biscuits	Brainy Bliss Balls
Supper	Pumpkin Seed Pesto and Lentil Chicken Nuggets with Rosemary & Garlic Chips	Supercharged Beef & Lentil Ragu with Spaghetti and broccoli florets	Tahini, Mustard & Tarragon Chicken Thighs with Cheesy Mashed Sweet Potato and cauliflower florets

THURSDAY	FRIDAY	SATURDAY	SUNDAY
Apple & Cinnamon Overnight Oats	Eggy Salmon & Dill Muffins with Mango, Avocado & Chia Pudding	Blueberry & Banana Baked Oats	Cheesy Courgette Waffles with Strawberry, Peach & Almond Pudding
Apple Doughnut Rings	Roasted Chickpea Bites, Italian Pizza Flavour	Cheesy Butterbean Bites	Spiced Crackers with an Orange Twist
Asian Prawn Fried Rice	Mini Sardine & Sweetcorn Quiches	Bean & Cheese Quesadilla	Barley & Pea Risotto/Arancini
Mini Avocado, Carrot & Blueberry Muffins	Marbled Berry Ice Lollies	Beets to the Rescue Bliss Balls	Raspberry & Mango Ice Lollies
Beefy Quinoa & Beetroot Burgers with Yellow Split Pea Flatbread and carrot batons	Fish Pie with Cheesy Potato & Broccoli Mash with peas	Mini Christmas Burgers	Lamb, Apricot & Cinnamon Tagine with Parsley Couscous

SHOPPING LIST

Some people like to buy just what they need for specific recipes, while others prefer to stock up on basic ingredients. Here is a list of goodies we often have in our fridge, freezer or store cupboard:

Fresh and frozen vegetables: broccoli, cabbage (red, white and spring), cauliflower, courgettes (zucchini), green beans, kale (and kalettes), mange tout, mushrooms, pak choi, peas, runner beans, sugar snap peas, spinach.

Root vegetables: carrots, celeriac, garlic, leeks, onions (white, red and spring), parsnips, potatoes (white, sweet and new), pumpkin, shallots, squash, swedes, turnips.

Salad: avocado, celery, cress, cucumber, fennel, lettuce (lamb's, Romaine, Little Gem), pea shoots, peppers (bell), radishes, rocket, spinach (baby leaf), tomato, watercress.

Fresh and frozen fruit: apples, apricots, bananas, blueberries, currants (red, black), cherries, grapes, kiwis, lemons, limes, mandarins, mangoes, melons (honeydew, cantaloupe, galia), nectarines, papayas, passionfruits, peaches, pears, pineapples, plums, pomegranates, oranges, raspberries, satsumas, strawberries, watermelons.

Dried fruit: apple rings, apricots (unsulphured), banana chips, cranberries (unsweetened), dates, figs, goji berries, mulberries, mangoes, prunes.

Healthy grains: barley, polenta (choose organic), couscous (wholegrain), farro, kamut, millet, oats, wheat (bulgur, freekah or wholemeal), rice (wholegrain brown, black, red or wild), spelt.

Noodles: pasta (wholemeal, spelt, buckwheat, chickpea, lentil, quinoa), noodles (brown rice, soba buckwheat).

Flours: spelt, buckwheat, chickpea (also known as besan/gram), Dove's Farm gluten-free, rye, ground almonds, coconut, quinoa, brown rice, wholemeal.

Baking ingredients: baking powder, bicarbonate of soda, xanthum gum, arrowroot.

Cereals: porridge oats, puffed brown rice, puffed quinoa, buckwheat flakes, millet flakes, brown rice flakes, coconut flakes.

Pseudo-grains: amaranth, buckwheat, millet, quinoa.

Beans and pulses: lentils (red, green, puy), beans (butter, flageolet, edamame, cannellini, black, mung, adzuki, kidney), chickpeas, yellow split peas; try legume rice and pasta.

Fish: line-caught mackerel, anchovies, sardines, wild or organic salmon, trout, cod, halibut; tinned and frozen fish and prawns.

Poultry and meat: organic/free-range poultry (chicken, turkey, duck, pheasant, partridge, guinea fowl), organic/free-range/grass-fed lamb, beef, pork, venison.

Broths and stocks: fresh meat/poultry/fish/vegetable stock; low-salt organic stock cubes.

Milk: organic full-fat cow's, goat's; oat milk, nut milks (coconut, almond, hazelnut, cashew), hemp milk.

Yoghurt: Greek, full-fat organic, kefir; nut alternatives (coconut, almond, cashew).

Cream: organic crème fraîche, organic cream, oat crème fraîche.

Cheese: organic cow's, goat's, sheep's; buffalo mozzarella, mascarpone, ricotta.

Eggs: organic free-range chicken's; quail, duck or goose.

Seeds: pumpkin, sunflower, hemp, chia, sesame, flax (linseed), poppy.

Nuts: almonds, pecans, brazils, hazelnuts, walnuts, pistachios, macademias, cashews, pine kernels, peanuts.

Nut and seed butters: peanut, hazelnut, cashew, almond, sunflower, pumpkin.

Healthy fats: coconut oil (kids prefer cooking coconut oils with a neutral flavour), olive oil (light and extra virgin), cold-pressed rapeseed oil, organic butter, avocado oil, goose fat, duck fat.

Natural sweeteners: honey (organic, Jarrah, Manuka, local or raw), maple syrup, coconut sugar, treacle (black strap molasses), date syrup, dates, vanilla essence, cinnamon, apple, pear or mango purée, mashed banana, stevia, xylitol.

Chocolate: dark 70% chocolate, raw cacao powder and nibs, carob, dairy-free brands.

Fresh and dried herbs: mint, parsley, coriander, rosemary, thyme, sage, oregano, basil, mixed Mediterranean herbs, Herbes de Provence.

Ground and whole spices: turmeric, black pepper, cumin, coriander, ginger, fenugreek, cardamom, cloves, sumac, paprika.

Seaweeds: nori, kombu, dulse, seaweed salad.

Salt: Himalayan pink, sea and celery salts.

Preserved foods: olives in olive oil or brine, capers, sun-dried tomatoes.

Condiments: miso, tahini, tamari soya sauce, organic tomato concentrate, mustard, Worcester sauce, organic mayonnaise, coconut aminos.

Vinegars: apple cider, balsamic, apple balsamic, red and white wine.

Superfood powders: acai, baobab, fruits (strawberry, raspberry, banana).

Hot drinks: herbal teas including chamomile, fresh mint, peppermint, ginger, liquorice and rooibos.

You should be able to source most of these foods in your local supermarket. However, some of the allergen-friendly and specialist foods may be a bit trickier to find and you can buy this online from NatureDoc Shop.

ENDNOTES

1. The Declaration of Nutrition, Health, and Intelligence for the Child-To-Be https://journals.sagepub.com/doi/10.1177/026010600701900212

2. Relationship Between Diet and Mental Health in Children and Adolescents: A Systematic Review https://www.ncbi.nlm.nih.gov/pmc/articles/PMC4167107/

3. Nutritional Psychiatry: Towards Improving Mental Health by What You Eat https://www.sciencedirect.com/science/article/pii/S0924977X19317237?via%3Dihub

4. A Causal Mechanism for Childhood Acute Lymphoblastic Leukaemia https://www.ncbi.nlm.nih.gov/pmc/articles/PMC6986894/

5. Healthy eating linked to kids' happiness https://www.sciencedaily.com/releases/2017/12/171213220122.htm

6. A Traditional Diet Is Associated with a Reduced Risk of Eczema and Wheeze in Colombian Children https://www.ncbi.nlm.nih.gov/pmc/articles/PMC4516989/

7. Effect of Diet and Maternal Education on Allergies Among Preschool Children: A Case-Control Study https://www.sciencedirect.com/science/article/abs/pii/S0013935117316031?via%3Dihub

8. The Role of Nutrition in Asthma Prevention and Treatment https://academic.oup.com/nutritionreviews/advance-article/doi/10.1093/nutrit/nuaa005/5804968

9. Children who don't like fruit and vegetables are 13 times more likely to be constipated https://www.sciencedaily.com/releases/2010/12/101213071111.htm

10. Are Dietary Patterns in Childhood Associated With IQ at 8 Years of Age? A Population-Based Cohort Study https://pubmed.ncbi.nlm.nih.gov/21300993/

11. Glycemic Index and Glycemic Load https://lpi.oregonstate.edu/mic/food-beverages/glycemic-index-glycemic-load

12. Whole Milk Compared With Reduced-Fat Milk and Childhood Overweight: A Systematic Review and Meta-Analysis https://pubmed.ncbi.nlm.nih.gov/31851302/

13. Associations Between Dairy Intake, Body Composition, and Cardiometabolic Risk Factors in Spanish Schoolchildren: The Cuenca Study https://www.mdpi.com/2072-6643/11/12/2940

14. Eggs and beyond: is dietary cholesterol no longer important? https://academic.oup.com/ajcn/article/102/2/235/4614547

15. Complementary Feeding and "Donner Les Bases Du Goût" (Providing the Foundation of Taste). A Qualitative Approach to Understand Weaning Practices, Attitudes and Experiences by French Mothers https://pubmed.ncbi.nlm.nih.gov/24045210/

16. Pesticide Exposure and Child Neurodevelopment https://www.ncbi.nlm.nih.gov/pmc/articles/PMC4247335/

17. Pesticide Exposure in Children https://pubmed.ncbi.nlm.nih.gov/23184105/

18. Diet and Contaminants: Driving the Rise to Obesity Epidemics? http://www.eurekaselect.com/152534/article

19. Pesticide Toxicity and the Developing Brain https://pubmed.ncbi.nlm.nih.gov/18226078/

20. Early-Life Exposure to Persistent Organic Pollutants (OCPs, PBDEs, PCBs, PFASs) and Attention-Deficit/Hyperactivity Disorder: A Multi-Pollutant Analysis of a Norwegian Birth Cohort https://www.sciencedirect.com/science/article/pii/S0160412018306810?via%3Dihub

21. Production-Related Contaminants (Pesticides, Antibiotics and Hormones) in Organic and Conventionally Produced Milk Samples Sold in the USA https://www.cambridge.org/core/journals/public-health-nutrition/article/productionrelated-contaminants-pesticides-antibiotics-and-hormones-in-organic-and-conventionally-produced-milk-samples-sold-in-the-usa/D1107FE30C778A73F5F601C5D3D6E572

22. Effectiveness of Commercial and Homemade Washing Agents in Removing Pesticide Residues on and in Apples https://www.ncbi.nlm.nih.gov/pubmed/29067814

23. Your baby's first solid foods https://www.nhs.uk/conditions/pregnancy-and-baby/solid-foods-weaning/

24. Clinical trials investigating how to best prevent Peanut Allergy http://www.leapstudy.co.uk/

25. Long-term Consequences of Early Fruit and Vegetable Feeding Practices in the United Kingdom https://pubmed.ncbi.nlm.nih.gov/20529400/

26. The Effects of Repeated Exposure to Garlic-Flavored Milk on the Nursling's Behavior https://pubmed.ncbi.nlm.nih.gov/8108198/

27. Zinc Content in Breast Milk and Its Association With Maternal Diet https://www.mdpi.com/2072-6643/10/10/1438

28. Concentrations of Water-Soluble Forms of Choline in Human Milk from Lactating Women in Canada and Cambodia https://www.ncbi.nlm.nih.gov/pmc/articles/PMC5872799/

29. Fish Intake Reflects on DHA Level in Breast Milk Among Lactating Women in Latvia https://pubmed.ncbi.nlm.nih.gov/30038661/

30. Botulism https://www.nhs.uk/conditions/botulism/

31. Low Omega-3 Index in Pregnancy Is a Possible Biological Risk Factor for Postpartum Depression https://www.ncbi.nlm.nih.gov/pmc/articles/PMC3701051/

32. Emerging Risk Factors for Postpartum Depression: Serotonin Transporter Genotype and Omega-3 Fatty Acid Status https://www.ncbi.nlm.nih.gov/pmc/articles/PMC5173356/

33. N-3 (Omega-3) Fatty Acids in Postpartum Depression: Implications for Prevention and Treatment https://www.ncbi.nlm.nih.gov/pmc/articles/PMC2989696/

34. Docosahexaenoic Acid https://www.karger.com/Article/FullText/448262

35. Human Milk Omega-3 Fatty Acid Composition Is Associated With Infant Temperament https://www.mdpi.com/2072-6643/11/12/2964

36. Efficiency of Conversion of Alpha-Linolenic Acid to Long Chain N-3 Fatty Acids in Man https://www.ncbi.nlm.nih.gov/pubmed/11844977

37. Effect of Inadequate Iodine Status in UK Pregnant Women on Cognitive Outcomes in Their Children: Results From the Avon Longitudinal Study of Parents and Children (ALSPAC) https://pubmed.ncbi.nlm.nih.gov/23706508/

38. Iodine Status and Growth In 0-2-Year-Old Infants With Cow's Milk Protein Allergy https://journals.lww.com/jpgn/Fulltext/2017/05000/Iodine_Status_and_Growth_In_0_2_Year_Old_Infants.29.aspx

39. UK Iodine Group https://www.ukiodine.org/faqs/

40. Vitamin B12 https://ods.od.nih.gov/factsheets/VitaminB12-HealthProfessional/

41. Choline: Critical Role During Fetal Development and Dietary Requirements in Adults https://www.ncbi.nlm.nih.gov/pmc/articles/PMC2441939/

42. The Fetal Origins of Memory: The Role of Dietary Choline in Optimal Brain Development https://pubmed.ncbi.nlm.nih.gov/17212955/

43. Choline The Underconsumed and Underappreciated Essential Nutrient https://www.ncbi.nlm.nih.gov/pmc/articles/PMC6259877/

44. Choline in anxiety and depression: the Hordaland Health Study https://academic.oup.com/ajcn/article/90/4/1056/4596992

45. Choline Supply of Preterm Infants: Assessment of Dietary Intake and Pathophysiological Considerations https://pubmed.ncbi.nlm.nih.gov/22961562/

46. AMA's stance on choline, prenatal vitamins could bring 'staggering' results https://www.researchgate.net/publication/319144119_AMA's_stance_on_choline_prenatal_vitamins_could_bring_'staggering'_results

47. Choline https://ods.od.nih.gov/factsheets/Choline-HealthProfessional/

48. Vitamin C and Immune Function https://www.ncbi.nlm.nih.gov/pubmed/19263912

49. Diagnosis and Management of Vitamin D Deficiency https://www.bmj.com/content/340/bmj.b5664.extract

50. Emphasizing the Health Benefits of Vitamin D for Those with Neurodevelopmental Disorders and Intellectual Disabilities https://www.ncbi.nlm.nih.gov/pmc/articles/PMC4377865/

51. Sunlight and Vitamin D. A Global Perspective for Health https://www.ncbi.nlm.nih.gov/pmc/articles/PMC3897598/

52. Vitamin D https://ods.od.nih.gov/factsheets/VitaminD-HealthProfessional/

53. Infants and elderlies are susceptible to zinc deficiency https://www.ncbi.nlm.nih.gov/pmc/articles/PMC4766432/

54. Zinc: An Overview https://www.ncbi.nlm.nih.gov/pubmed/7749260/

55. Zinc and the Special Senses https://www.ncbi.nlm.nih.gov/pubmed/6349457

56. Anemia and Iron Deficiency in Children: Association with Red Meat and Poultry Consumption https://www.ncbi.nlm.nih.gov/pubmed/24280989

57. Prevalence and Risk Factors of Anemia in Children https://www.ncbi.nlm.nih.gov/pubmed/26893206

58. Consumption of Cow's Milk as a Cause of Iron Deficiency in Infants and Toddlers https://pubmed.ncbi.nlm.nih.gov/22043881/

59. Iron Deficiency and Impaired Child Development https://www.ncbi.nlm.nih.gov/pmc/articles/PMC1121846/

60. Impact of Iron Deficiency Anemia on the Function of the Immune System in Children https://www.ncbi.nlm.nih.gov/pubmed/27893677

61. Iron and Learning Potential in Childhood https://www.ncbi.nlm.nih.gov/pmc/articles/PMC1807911/

62. Iron Needs of Babies and Children https://www.ncbi.nlm.nih.gov/pmc/articles/PMC2528681/

63. Role of the Human Breast Milk-Associated Microbiota on the Newborns' Immune System: A Mini Review https://www.ncbi.nlm.nih.gov/pmc/articles/PMC5661030/

64. Cells of Human Breast Milk https://www.ncbi.nlm.nih.gov/pmc/articles/PMC5508878/

65. Does the Use of Antibiotics in Early Childhood Increase the Risk of Asthma and Allergic Disease? https://pubmed.ncbi.nlm.nih.gov/11069562/

66. Antibiotic Use in Children With Asthma: Cohort Study in UK and Dutch Primary Care Databases https://bmjopen.bmj.com/content/8/11/e022979

67. Does Early Life Exposure to Antibiotics Increase the Risk of Eczema? A Systematic Review https://onlinelibrary.wiley.com/doi/abs/10.1111/bjd.12476

68. Association Between Exposure to Antimicrobial Household Products and Allergic Symptoms https://www.ncbi.nlm.nih.gov/pmc/articles/PMC4243727/

69. Too Clean, or not Too Clean: the Hygiene Hypothesis and Home Hygiene https://www.ncbi.nlm.nih.gov/pmc/articles/PMC1448690/

70. The Rapidly Changing World of Food Allergy in Children https://www.ncbi.nlm.nih.gov/pmc/articles/PMC4371379/

71. Food Allergy in Childhood https://www.ncbi.nlm.nih.gov/pubmed/17014410

72. Nut allergy https://patient.info/health/food-allergy-and-intolerance/nut-allergy

73. Peanut, Milk, and Wheat Intake During Pregnancy is Associated with Reduced Allergy and Asthma in Children https://www.ncbi.nlm.nih.gov/pubmed/24522094

74. Sugar Intake in Pregnancy is Linked to Child's Allergy and Allergic Asthma https://www.bmj.com/content/358/bmj.j3293.full

75. Probiotics for the Prevention of Allergy: A Systematic Review and Meta-Analysis of Randomized Controlled Trials https://www.ncbi.nlm.nih.gov/pubmed/26044853

76. Prevention of Asthma and Allergic Diseases in Children https://www.ncbi.nlm.nih.gov/pubmed/12829339

77. The Role of the Microbial Environment for the Development of Childhood Asthma and Allergies https://www.ncbi.nlm.nih.gov/pubmed/24297856

78. Establishing the Prevalence of Low Vitamin D in Non-Immunoglobulin-E Mediated Gastrointestinal Food Allergic Children in a Tertiary Centre https://www.ncbi.nlm.nih.gov/pubmed/28101293

79. Vegan Nutrition for Mothers and Children: Practical Tools for Healthcare Providers https://pubmed.ncbi.nlm.nih.gov/30577451/

ACKNOWLEDGEMENTS

Writing a cookbook during a global pandemic has had its challenges, and I can't thank Rebecca Nicolson, Aurea Carpenter, Katherine Stroud and Becke Parker at Short Books enough for keeping calm all the way.

Huge thanks also go out to Alex and Emma Smith, Jo Roberts-Miller and Lola Milne for transforming the recipes into beautiful images and making this book totally shine. You are an awesome team!

I have also loved involving some of my NatureDoc clinical team. Marion Boulter you are a total gem and thank you for being at my side right from the start – it's been so much fun. Thank you also to your boys Archie and Edward for being so great on the cover and for eating all those raspberries! Also, thanks to Jo Saunders for coming out with your gorgeous brood Max, Molly and Mary on the coldest day of the year to eat ice lollies! And thanks to Katy Gordon-Smith for lending us your beautiful kitchen and to her sweet Martha and Miles.

The babies were totally adorable and thankfully scoffed all the food. Alfie, Imogen, Hugo, Arthur, Silvia, Emidi, Emiko and Louis, you were total stars. And thanks to Hattie Hathaway and Sarah Stevenson for helping put us in touch with some of them.

Thanks also to the gang of mini food critics who tested my recipes from their kitchens all over the UK and further afield, and to their parents for giving me the best feedback, as I haven't had a baby myself for quite a while!

My family have been incredible, too, and luckily lockdown meant they were always at the ready to be champion food tasters themselves, proving that the recipes really are not just for babies. Thank you darlings Christopher, Barney, Lara and Charlie, I really couldn't have done this without you. And to my Daddy and Catriona for being there all the way with buckets of encouragement.

ABOUT THE AUTHOR

Lucinda Miller is the NatureDoc. She is the UK's go-to naturopath and child nutrition expert and runs a nutritional therapy clinical team specialising in mother and child nutrition. She works alongside paediatricians, child neurologists and child psychiatrists using a truly integrated approach to health. Lucinda writes a blog at www.naturedoc.co.uk, offering simple and effective tips for brighter, happier children, as well as a recipe resource, dedicated to delicious and healthy recipes for tricky diets. She has been practising as a naturopath for over 20 years and has also qualified in Functional Medicine and is a Master Herbalist. She is a mum of three and lives in Wiltshire. Her bestselling first cookbook *The Good Stuff* was published by Short Books in September 2018.

'Lucinda has totally changed my family's health for the better. This cookbook is full of amazingly delicious and healthy recipes you can all enjoy.'
LEONORA BAMFORD, MY BABA

'Aimed at maximising development whilst ensuring that eating becomes a social event devoid of stress, Lucinda's latest book guides parents down an exciting path of healthy eating for children, with a sprinkle of fun added!'
DR TIM UBHI, THE CHILDREN'S E-HOSPITAL